COME HOME, SAILOR

Also by Eric Kemp:
  – Captain John Kemp MBE –
  A Master Mariner of the 20th Century
  Yes Dad, I Want to Go to Sea!

Come Home, Sailor

Eric Kemp

UNITED WRITERS
Cornwall

UNITED WRITERS PUBLICATIONS LTD
Ailsa, Castle Gate, Penzance, Cornwall.

British Library Cataloguing in Publication Data:
A catalogue record for this book is
available from the British Library.

ISBN 9781852001728

Printed in Great Britain by
United Writers Publications Ltd
Cornwall.

I dedicate this book to
the St. Ives Lifeboat Station,
and those who helped me in
the service of both Mount's Bay
and St. Ives Bay Pilotages.
Also to my wife Jillian and
sons Ian and Jeremy.

Acknowledgements

I firmly believe that most people have within them a good book of experiences taken from their working life. In my case I have been lucky in being able to write about both my father's life and my own in three books, of which this is the third.

I particularly wish to express my thanks to my wife, who has helped with the proof-reading of each book. However, I would put on record one disagreement between us in this matter. I, in all my years at sea, have always called a ship 'her' or 'she'. My wife, a former teacher of Religious Education and English, says a ship is an inanimate object. Jill has argued that, as I wish to reach those people not used to the ways of the sea with my books, I should not use the female term. I make my apologies to my seafaring friends, but to keep the peace I have agreed to follow Jill's advice, of course!

I also wish to record my appreciation for the help given by my two sons Ian and Jeremy, as well as the owners of some of the photographs who have allowed me to publish their work in this book; and finally I thank my publisher for all his advice and help in this task.

Contents

1

A Port Relieving Officer

In July 1960 I was about to get married, and the long voyages I was undertaking in The Ellerman Shipping Company, for which I was working at that time, were not to my liking. I was planning for a more settled life at sea, so I joined the Palm Line, attracted by the shorter voyages to West Africa and the additional benefit of better pay and leave.

By July 1965 I had served five years of very hard labour working long hours on visits to West Africa. These voyages were spread between ports from Dakar in the north, to Luanda and Lobito in the south. Sixteen hour working days were not uncommon on these voyages; and with officers sweating in the tropical heat of West Africa it was very stressful work. Also the advent of countries such as Ghana, Nigeria and Sierra Leone becoming independent added to the difficulties.

In all I was to serve on fourteen of the company's ships, ranging from the ageing *Ashanti Palm* to the modern *Lobito Palm*. By 1965 I had gained my Master's Foreign Going Certificate – and my four year old son Ian was growing up seeing very little of his father.

I still wanted a career at sea, but also wished to spend much more time with my family. My wife Jill encouraged me in this and so, at the end of September, I left the Palm Line with little regret. I then applied for a job as second officer in the Trinity

House Steam Vessel Service. There was, however, a waiting list, and I would have to be available in the United Kingdom immediately a vacancy occurred.

Taking advice from the Merchant Navy Officers Association I obtained temporary work on the coast during the second week of September. In fact, I took a position as a port relieving officer with the Blue Star Line. My conditions of employment enabled me to resign at a week's notice should a vacancy come up with Trinity House. So, with the prospect of serving this well respected shipping line, I returned to St. Ives to await my first appointment.

At the time I was very keen to see if their ships were as good as they looked. Fulfilment of my wish was not long in coming, as the next day I was asked to join the MV *Sydney Star*; then in dry dock undergoing repairs at the Wallsend Shipyard on the River Tyne near Newcastle.

On arrival I was soon to find out that there were snags to my new appointment; but as it was only temporary I was willing to put up with a lack of heating and crew! The ship was acclaimed for taking part in the famous Malta Convoy known as 'Operation Substance' in July 1941. At that time the vessel was one of six fast liners escorted by no less than 25 warships, including a battleship, a battle cruiser, an aircraft carrier, a fast minelayer, 4 cruisers and 17 destroyers, all working to provide the Maltese with much needed supplies in the desperate wartime situation.

Under the command of Captain T.S. Horn the vessel had been hit by a torpedo and seriously damaged, leaving a forty foot by sixteen foot hole in the ship's side. Despite having to evacuate 400 troops on board to a destroyer, the captain and crew continued the journey in tow by one of the warships, and under great difficulty delivered the cargo to Malta.

Built by the Harland and Wolf shipyard in Belfast in 1936, by the time I joined the *Sydney Star* it was 29 years old and getting very near to the end of its useful life. The vessel had suffered a bad galley fire, numerous breakdowns, and been under repair in dock for over three months for a so-called refit.

One cabin on the ship had been kept fairly habitable, and when I climbed aboard I found another 2nd officer waiting impatiently for my arrival. He was leaving to study for his Master's Certificate and had served over a month while a relief was found. The handover did not take very long. He informed me that the ship and the *New Zealand Star,* berthed in South Shields and also having a refit, were both under the control of a chief officer based close by. The chief officer would visit the ship twice a week with any orders and also get any stores I needed. The *Sydney Star* had power supplied from the shore and, as well as giving light and heat to my cabin, this allowed the accommodation and working parts of the ship to be well lit when required. I was supposed to sleep ashore but could stay aboard if I wished. This proved very acceptable as the pay was poor and £40 a week was allowed for my food and shoreside accommodation.

I soon had a look around the ship, noting the store rooms and navigational systems, as well as fire equipment. Each morning during the working week I would meet the workers coming aboard and help them in any way needed – such as getting portable lights to illuminate dark areas in the ship. I quickly discovered that there was a very great deal of work that had to be finished to complete the refit.

The ship was built to carry general and refrigerated cargoes and employed a very large number of engineers and electricians; some 13 in all. A few looked after the very large freezing spaces, while others tended engines and machinery. These were checked daily, together with all the crew and passenger accommodation, for health and safety reasons. Each day, therefore, I would patrol right through the vessel checking for fires and any other problems that might occur. Just the same, I had a lot of time to spare and I was soon to put it to good use.

On the Friday before my second weekend aboard, the chief officer arrived with the news that the ship repairers would be working on Sundays in future to speed up the refit. This was necessary to get the ship into operation as soon as possible. I was consequently required to help with the lights and fire watch, etc., while the dockyard workers were on board. This I carried out without comment and all went well over the first weekend.

On the Monday, after boarding the ship, my senior officer

complimented me on the work, saying that the shipyard management was impressed at the help they had received. As a reward, and in recognition of my help, the company would increase my wages by a half day's pay.

Now, as it happened, I was a paid up member of the Navigating Officers' Union and had attended one of the Annual Conferences as a delegate. So, knowing the Merchant Navy shipping act, I claimed a full day's wages as I had actually worked twelve hours on that Sunday. Much to my annoyance I was told I was a port relieving officer, and as such had no rights to such payments anyway. That was something I was not willing to accept, so using the old ship's typewriter (with one finger, at first) I wrote protesting to my union. The union repeated the news given to me by my superior officer.

Bearing in mind the unfairness of the situation I entered into a five week correspondence with the union. Each time I received a reply I would write another protesting letter.

Eventually, after I had left the company, the union wrote to me at home to congratulate me for winning a rise for all port relieving officers (except myself, of course, as I had moved on). Nevertheless, by then I had taught myself to type and in doing this had passed the time very usefully!

2

A Coastal Voyage to Remember

Eventually life began to return to the *Sydney Star*. By the second week of October a new generator had been lowered into the engine room, the galley had received its cooking apparatus repaired and returned, the much repaired engines were given a run alongside the berth, and a full crew had joined.

It's over forty-seven years ago, but I believe it was Captain Fuland who took command, and I can remember his worried frown as he talked about the state of the ship and its seaworthiness for the coastal voyage around Scotland. Both the shipyard manager and the captain tried to delay our departure in order to test the repairs already made and complete those still underway. The company superintendent, however, insisted that all repairs would be completed in Liverpool by their own dockyard workers.

"All you have to do, Captain," he said, "is to get the vessel to the loading berth in Liverpool and we can catch up on the schedule while the vessel is repaired."

In hindsight this was a decision which turned out to be very unwise and endangered the ship.

So on the 22nd of October 1965 at 8am in the morning, *Sydney Star,* with a Pilot on board, slipped the moorings at Wallsend, then proceeded down the River Tyne, past the *New Zealand Star* at South Shields, and out into the North Sea to complete trials.

15

Following completion of these, the pilot disembarked and we set off northwards towards Liverpool.

Trouble was not long in coming, and just a half hour later, as the accommodation lights went out and the ship's engines slowed, the new generator failed. Our chief engineer had just passed his chief engineer's certificate and it was to be a baptism of near disaster over the next twenty-four hours for him.

This first failure was sorted out quite quickly, and it did not take too long before some power was restored with the reserve generator which started with a rumble. After a consultation with the chief engineer, the captain reported to the company superintendent who advised him to proceed and that repairs would be carried out in Liverpool.

The Blue Star Company did not provide a radar set for their vessels, and therefore the *Sydney Star* officers could only know of approaching vessels by their fog sirens in bad visibility. There was a position fixing system called the Decca Navigator and we could check on the chart where we were at all times, but in fog we could not see other ships approaching.

Following the temporary loss of power, the ship's Sperry Gyro Compass ceased to work and just swung around in endless circles. As this piece of equipment was my responsibility, I had to spend the next two hours down below attempting to return this electronic apparatus to working order. Meanwhile the ship was using a magnetic compass to proceed.

I did eventually find that a small piece of the works in the compass had fallen out of position and I was thus able to repair it. So it was 7pm before I was able to turn in to my bunk and get some sleep in advance of relieving Paul Milner, the ship's 3rd officer. As I fell asleep the ship was surging ahead at 18 knots towards the Pentland Firth on passage round the north of the Scottish mainland.

However, on waking and climbing to the bridge to begin my watch at midnight, I could hear that we had run into more trouble. The ship was now proceeding at half speed in thick fog and the moaning of the fog signal was booming away into the darkness every two minutes.

Paul was a cheerful fellow and explained that we were now approaching Cape Wrath and would soon be heading southwards passing the Outer Hebrides. "There was some trouble with the starboard engine," he told me, "and we had to stop it for an hour with a scavenge fire. Now you will have to be on your guard and listen for approaching vessels."

The captain, sitting in his tall chair, made no comment as we sailed on into the fog.

During the next three hours we were to experience three more scavenge fires affecting both engines – our progress slowed considerably. Two vessels passed us, proceeding in the opposite direction, but we could only hear them and it was an anxious time. Then, in the last hour of the watch, we received a severe south-west gale warning for our area. By 4am the fog had cleared and the wind was strengthening rapidly as I returned to my cabin to resume the rest of my night's sleep.

The steward called me at 7.45am with a cup of tea as I would have to relieve Paul at 8.30am for his meal break. I could immediately tell something was wrong because the ship was rolling violently.

The steward announced grimly: "This cup of tea will be the only hot thing you'll get today."

"What's wrong?" I asked.

"Power has just failed and we are very near a lighthouse on rocks sir."

Grabbing a couple of sandwiches from the saloon I quickly made my way up to the bridge. The situation that came into sight was alarming, to say the least. Just two miles away, with waves breaking white against the grey sea, was the dramatic sight of the Skerryvore Lighthouse, 160 feet high and marking a highly dangerous reef of rocks.

The *Sydney Star* lay almost stopped by a fast running tide and the fierce south-west wind. The starboard engine was stopped while another scavenge fire was being extinguished, and the port engine was only working at dead slow speed ahead. With the ship's wheel at hard to starboard we were just about able to hold her position, but very slowly drifting towards the lighthouse.

I must admit the captain's face looked grey as he called me over to his high chair placed close to the helmsman steering the vessel.

"Now Second, you can see our position, go down to the engine room and ask the chief how long he is going to be. I know things are pretty bad but we do need to get round the lighthouse and into the open sea. Repairs will not be much use if we go aground on the rocks."

"Yes sir," I said, keen to help given the predicament that we were in.

I must admit I was not prepared for what I was about to experience. The entrance to the engine room was sighted on deck near to the base of the funnel and very close to the lifeboat deck. Standing close by were a number of stewards wearing their life jackets, and I remarked: "What is wrong with you lot, there are no orders to don life jackets?"

They replied: "You wait until you open that engine room door."

As I entered, smoke was coming from the starboard engine and the paintwork along the side of both engines was blackened and blistered. The ladder I was standing on was slippery with oil and above the noise of the one working engine I could hear (as I was to find out later) 300 tons of water moving around beneath the steel deck plates under the engines. This sea water had entered the ship by way of badly fitted propeller shafts.

The engineers at this time had to monitor the bearings under the propeller shafts and the watertight door protecting the engine room could not be closed. At the controls of the working engine the 3rd engineer struggled hard to keep it at a constant rate of revolutions as the vessel moved about in the very rough seas. The chief engineer was standing forward of the engines watching the rest of the engineers and electricians coping with faults in two fuel oil separators. Normally the engines could work with just one of these but now both had failed, and the engines could only be run at dead slow speed. Now, with the ship moving and rolling in all directions, they were struggling to shift one oil separator from its normal position to the position of the other failed machine.

This was indeed a very hazardous operation with all the men in danger of serious injury.

As I expected, I was not to get a big welcome from the chief engineer. Indeed, if I repeated what was said it would have very much annoyed our captain. However, I was able to tell him of our problems on the bridge and he rapidly calmed down.

"I know, Second," he said, "tell the captain that I will give you emergency full ahead if the ship gets too close to the rocks." (As it happened it would not have been a great deal of use, we would still not be clear of danger near the rocky shore if the engines failed.) "As for completion I am doing my best, believe me."

I must admit I could only agree, and climbed back up to the deck trying to look confident as I passed the stewards still wearing their life jackets.

Back on the bridge we were to spend a worrying couple of hours. The very slow drift of the vessel continued, so by 11am we were just one and a half miles from the rocks.

Then, just as we were getting really worried, the tide turned and the ship began to change its heading and steam into the wind. This meant that the severe rolling motion of the ship eased, and with a great effort the engineers succeeded in getting the parts of the two separators together on the starboard side. By 11.30am the two useless machines had become one working separator.

From that point it took only minutes for the engines to speed up and at 12 knots we steamed away from our dangerous position. The engineers were also able to get some more power from one of the generators, so that the ship's pumps could reduce the water entering the ship through the propeller shafts.

By the early afternoon the captain was considering proceeding to the port of Londonderry in Northern Ireland for necessary repairs. However, at this point, with the gale rapidly easing, we received a worrying weather forecast: the calm period of weather would be followed by a storm force north-westerly gale. So with the engines working, it made good sense to try and get to Liverpool while the good weather held. To this end we had to proceed to a position off Point Lynas in North Wales, where we could get the assistance of a Liverpool Pilot. This was to cause us

19

a further problem, as the chief engineer pointed out that if we stopped the engines he was not sure of starting them again.

Point Lynas, near the Isle of Anglesey, is very exposed to north-west gales and the wind would be blowing towards the shore if we could not proceed. However, we had to have a pilot and the company superintendent ordered six harbour tugs to leave their positions on the river Mersey in Liverpool and stand by to help should they be needed. At the pilot station the captain decided to drop the ship's anchor so that if the engines were to fail we would have time to accept help from the tugs.

Indeed it did take the engineers an hour to get the engine going again, but our luck held and we were eventually able to get into the riverside lock, and from there into the dock system just before midnight.

Next morning I was in for a real surprise. The first workers to board our vessel were dockers to load general cargo for New Zealand. It seemed the repairs were a much lower priority than loading the ship.

It was now that the company asked the 3rd officer Paul and myself if we would sail with the ship on the coming voyage. We both had a chat about it during the morning break for coffee. I had no intention of going in any case, but Paul was a company man and to refuse had implications for his future. He showed me where the deck above his cabin wardrobe had worn so thin that it had let in seawater which had ruined his best uniform. With the state of the ship being so poor he too decided not to go – so together we informed the company of our decision.

With hindsight I have often wondered if Paul's life could have been very different. As it was, I told the company superintendent that I would be watching the marine movement lists in the Lloyds Journal to see where the ship would be visiting ports for repairs.

It turned out that, after sailing, the vessel had a major breakdown in the Mediterranean and stayed in Malta for some time. The ship then proceeded to Colombo in Ceylon, where a fire broke out in Number 4 hold and caused the death of the 2nd officer who had relieved me.

3

The Tragic Death of
Our Third Officer

We spent a further week aboard the *Sydney Star* before being transferred to the *New Zealand Star* which was then still in South Shields.

Paul and I left the *Sydney Star* together and stopped off at his home outside Leeds to spend a very pleasant twenty-four hour break with his family. From there we travelled on to South Shields and our next voyage around the north of Scotland.

Thankfully this vessel was in much better condition. Although, in fact, the *New Zealand Star* at 10,940 gross tons was a sister ship to the ill-fated *Sydney Star,* and also built at Harland and Wolf shipyard in Belfast in 1935.

After a pleasant week in South Shields, followed by engine and equipment trials, we left once more to travel north around Scotland, bound for Glasgow and Liverpool to load for Australia.

This time the weather was much better and the ship made a fast voyage to the Clyde. There the cargo to be loaded included a large consignment of whisky and other general cargo including cases of beer.

We arrived on a Friday and at once we found that it was to be no easy task loading so much booze. The ship had enough secure space to load the whisky but the beer was packed into the general cargo carried in the ship's open spaces within the five hatches.

The dockers had a very simple way of stealing the brew. They would drop the cases and drink the leaking liquid. To complicate things further the captain allowed the first and third officers to proceed on weekend leave along with one of the two apprentices. So, as second officer, I was left with just one apprentice to back up the shore watchmen (some of whom were afraid of reprisals if they reported men for theft). So it turned out that the two of us watched the whisky spaces and were not able to properly watch the cargo in open stow in the holds. By the end of each day the dockers were a very merry bunch as they left the ship. To us it represented a nightmare, as men under the influence could easily have very bad, if not fatal, accidents. Eventually we got through the weekend, but I was looking forward to seeing Paul on Monday as cargo loading resumed.

Very sadly, by eleven in the morning Paul had not appeared and I was stunned to be called up to the captain's cabin to be told that, driving a hired car, he had suffered a fatal accident in a two car crash on the English border while travelling home.

It was a sombre time as I packed up Paul's possessions and had them dispatched to Leeds. Shortly after we sailed to Liverpool and began loading the rest of a large cargo for Australia. While there the captain asked me to represent the ship at Paul's funeral. So I arranged a collection, bought a beautiful wreath, and travelled to Leeds in mid-November 1965, the day before his internment.

As I did not want to disturb the family at such a time, on arrival at Leeds station I hired a taxi. I asked the driver to find me accommodation before attending the funeral next day. So began a three mile journey from one guest house to another, while the meter ran on. At each one I was told that there were no vacancies because the following day was a fair day and all accommodation was full. At last I confronted a rather plump landlady who started our conversation with the familiar phrase: "It's all very difficult, you know."

I replied, "Yes, I am aware of the situation, but I'm getting desperate, madam."

"Well," she said slowly, winding me up even more, "I do have one room but there is a snag."

"Yes?" I said, not daring to hope.

"Well, it's the honeymoon suite and it costs a higher price, sir."

"Madam," I replied, "I don't care about the price, I am on expenses."

So the deal was done, but you can imagine my surprise when I discovered that the room held three beds! Just the same, I was too grateful for a bed to ask any awkward questions.

Next day I arrived at Paul's house and tried to comfort his family as best I could. However, I soon discovered that the Blue Star Office had failed to send a wreath. Fortunately I was able to insert the company's name on the ship's wreath I myself had bought and so avoid any bad feeling. Following the funeral service I was to spend time with the family in the Yorkshire countryside before returning to Liverpool.

On my arrival back at the ship the captain sent for me and was full of apologies for the company not sending a wreath. I was pleased to assure him and the company that the ship's wreath had the Blue Star name written on it by me. This greatly impressed the personnel department and, much to my surprise, they granted me a week's leave to which I was not really entitled. It was to prove a very fortunate break for me.

4

Trinity House Steam Vessel Service

On my arrival home the following day, I received a call from Captain Thompson, Trinity House Superintendent at Harwich in Essex. If I was able to join one of the Trinity House tenders the very next day, I could be appointed for a trial six month period as a relieving junior second officer.

After a quick call to the Blue Star office finishing my appointment with them, I was able to confirm to the Trinity House superintendent that I could travel. So it was that I received the news I was to join the fleet tender THV *Vestal* at Harwich. Following this appointment for two weeks, I would be relieving other officers on one of the nine tenders in the fleet. These were based at Harwich (4 ships), Great Yarmouth, Cowes, Penzance, Swansea and Holyhead.

I arrived in Harwich on a Friday evening to find the duty officer waiting to go home for the weekend. "Hi," he said cheerfully, "as you are away from home would you mind looking after the ship for the weekend? The steward will prepare your meals and you can go ashore any time, but stay close to the ship." Being new to the service of course I agreed, and I spent an undisturbed couple of days getting acquainted with the ship.

The Trinity House Vessel *Vestal* was built in Bristol in 1947 with a gross tonnage of 1,920 tons. The design was a very sturdy one along the lines used by the Royal Navy for corvettes

Eric Kemp.

Working boat from THV *Stella*. Nabo with the boat hook,
Junior 2nd Officer Jawdy, Coxswain Selwyn Jolly, plus others
at Longships Lighthouse, 1967.

Completing relief of Seven Stones Light Vessel, 1967.

At the Longships Lighthouse, 1969.
THV *Stella* in the background.

The *Torrey Canyon* wreck.

St. Ives Town Council Church Parade, 1971.
Eric Kemp 6th from front left column.

Queen of the Isles at St. Ives.

Tall ship *Sagres* pictured at the start of the 1970 race.
Taken by Frank Gibson from the *Queen of the Isles*.

Eric on the bridge of *Queen of the Isles*
alongside Liverpool Bar Light Vessel, 1970.

Collier MV *Garda Knight* arriving in Penzance
Dock, 1972. (Right down the middle!)

The complete Belgian Navy in Mount's Bay, 1975

Ship's agent Del Johnson at Penzance office.

Ship's agent Phil Westren at Penzance office.

Launching the St. Ives lifeboat *Frank Penfold Marshall*
at low water, circa 1970.

Irish vessel *Owen Bawn*, 248ft long.
The largest ship ever to enter Penzance Dry Dock.

escorting convoys across the Atlantic during World War Two. As well as two lifeboats the vessel carried two heavy duty workboats; in which I was about to get a baptism in seamanship. This would determine my suitability for an oncoming role in the Steam Vessel Service. On the foredeck the mast was rigged with a very large derrick, capable of lifting the largest of light buoys marking the channels around our coast. These were lifted on board, cleaned, repaired, repainted and recharged with gas bottles to keep the light working for months at a time. The bridge had the latest navigation equipment to check that the position of the buoy marking a danger or channel was correct.

Below the crew accommodation were 25 bunks and resting places for lightship crews in transit to their light vessels or lighthouses. In the ship's hold bags of coal were stored alongside portable pumps, water and fuel tanks. These items would be carried in the two workboats and stores of fuel oil, water, and coal would then be placed on the light vessel or lighthouse as well as transferring crews and food during a change over relief.

Monday morning came in due course and the crew arrived at 8am, while the officers strolled on board at 9am, to start their week's work. To me it seemed a paradise compared to the hours of working in the humidity of West Africa. By 10am we were on our way to Great Yarmouth to embark light vessel crews for a North Sea relief the following day. Outside Harwich the wind was blowing a north-west gale and in the shelter of the land *Vestal* made rapid progress northwards.

Just after our midday meal we received a message from the superintendent at Great Yarmouth to proceed to the South Leman light buoy, approximately 36 nautical miles off the Lincolnshire coast and close to the first BP oil and gas drilling rig Sea Gem. The buoy in question was unlit and needed checking and relighting. So we passed by Great Yarmouth and sailed on towards the extinguished light buoy position.

As the *Vestal* passed the shelter of the land south of Cromer in Norfolk the full effect of the storm and wind began to have an increasing impact on the ship, causing it to move violently as the swell increased from the north-west.

25

I was keeping watch on the bridge at the time when Captain Tarrant appeared at my side.

"I will be quite frank with you Kemp," he began, "deep sea sailors are usually unsuitable for this service and don't last very long."

Not wishing to offend I said nothing.

"Now you should accompany the senior second officer Roy Fiander in the workboat, but you need not go if you do not fancy the risk."

I was moved by this remark to answer: "I was brought up in St. Ives, sir, and I have been out in our fishing boats in worse weather than this, and I was further trained in the handling of small boats on the training ship HMS *Worcester* and will be perfectly willing to go."

"Right then, Kemp, we shall see what you are worth," he replied.

One hour later I was standing in the workboat which had been lowered to the boat deck level. The ship had arrived close to the buoy and within clear sight of the oil rig Sea Gem. The ship slowed in the seaway and turned across the swell, and I have always believed that Captain Tarrant let that happen deliberately, as now the *Vestal* began to roll from side to side in the prevailing weather conditions.

Many of the crew had turned out in the late afternoon to see how the new man reacted. The boat was cleared of restraints and swung out clear of the ship and dropped rapidly towards the turbulent sea. However, as this happened *Vestal* rolled the other way, swinging the boat violently into the ship's side before bouncing off and dropping into the sea. Our crew men, well used to this manoeuvre, quickly slipped the heavy blocks and wires holding the boat. Then we were free in the water and proceeding to the buoy. Meanwhile the coxswain and Roy were watching me very closely indeed.

"What did you think of that, then?" asked Roy.

"Exciting," I replied.

As we reached the buoy I could see that it was moving up and down by approximately ten feet or so and it was green with weed and had a very slippery surface. Now Roy gave me some very good advice.

"Eric, you are still in your merchant navy uniform and there is little point in getting it soiled. Just watch from the boat and see how you feel about doing it yourself in the next few weeks."

So I agreed, and watched Roy and one of the crew carry out the job of repairing the extinguished light buoy.

Then followed a testing hour's work, as first the gas pipe line had to be disconnected from the two bottles housed in the structure of the buoy, then a small bottle had to be fixed to the structure and the pipe line reconnected to the light, then relit and retimed. These actions restored its correct number of flashes in a fixed time so that passing mariners could identify it. This part of the operation proved difficult, because the crew of the nearby gas rig had been shooting at the structure with air rifles, causing the gas from the buoy to escape. As it happened, in five years with Trinity House, I was never to experience this particular problem again.

Finally, as the boat surged up against the buoy, the two men stepped lightly onto the deck area, and the boat then dropped ten feet in the next second or two. We were soon back at the ship which was once more rolling heavily, and it was quite difficult to hitch the blocks carrying the lifting wires into the lifting hooks. Following that the winch above could only raise the heavy 5 ton boat at a fairly slow pace, causing it to bump several times into the ship's side.

On reaching the level of the boat deck we were able to step aboard the ship once more. Waiting there as a spectator was the third engineer Kenneth Kessel, a fellow Cornishman. His cheery remark showed just how much attention there was to my first working boat trip.

"Seasick were you, Eric?" he said with a grin on his face, "never mind, pork for our meal tonight you know."

I replied, "Just the job, Ken, looking forward to it."

Up on the bridge Captain Tarrant was to have little to say but I knew he did not like my presence on board.

Late that evening we anchored off Great Yarmouth, and next

morning the two working boats went into the port and returned with relief crews and their stores to deliver to the various North Sea light vessels. Each of the lightships were made fast with a mooring rope from *Vestal*'s bow to their stern. Then the transfer of crews, stores, oil, water and coal began.

By Friday morning we were back alongside at Harwich and by the evening I was looking after the ship while the officers and crew were away home for the weekend. This was luxury when compared with the very hard work I had endured on my deep sea voyages around the world.

During my six month probation period I managed to travel around the various districts of Trinity House responsibility. I did get home for Christmas that year, though. Afterwards I relieved Garry, the junior second officer of the Trinity House Vessel *Stella* – 1500 gross tons, berthed at Penzance in Cornwall. I was to relieve on the ship on four more occasions in the first five months of 1966, before being appointed as the permanent second officer.

Oh what joy to be a mariner based in Cornwall and get home during most weeks and weekends as well as on my twenty-eight days' leave a year.

5

Service on THV *Stella*

It was during this period in January that my second son Jeremy was born, and I was to have the honour of helping the midwife with the birth.

Later that day my parents took my eldest son out so that we could have a quiet time for Jill to recover. Jeremy was resting in his cot when Ian was brought back home and I can well remember his reaction to his brother: "Hasn't grown much, has he?" summed up his opinion.

Commander Parsons was the captain of THV *Stella* when I joined her for the first time just after Christmas 1965. To say he was unconventional as a captain would not be an understatement. I had first met him when the chief engineer Mr Herbert Hawke, (a relative of mine) invited me on a voyage to relieve one of the keepers on the Wolf Rock Lighthouse, some 7 miles south of Land's End, in 1953. At that time the vessel based at Penzance was the THV *Satellite*, but now some twelve years later, although the vessel had changed, Captain Parsons was still there. He was a small chubby man, going slightly bald and apt to make decisions which finally caused him quite a lot of problems.

Shortly before I joined on this occasion, Porky (as the crew called their captain) had declined to enter harbour during Christmas Eve on the early morning tide saying the weather was too bad. The Penzance harbour master Ivor Gage would have normally placed two wooden booms on the dock gates sealing and closing the port until the weather had abated. As it was Christmas he had kept the harbour open at some risk to the gates.

After the high water had passed and the gates were closed, he told Commander Parsons that he would open once more on the evening tide, but if *Stella* did not enter then he would close the port for the rest of the holiday.

A mutiny then broke out in the crew accommodation and Commander Parsons was forced to face the men and explain his reasons. After a lot of straight talking, it was agreed the vessel should enter port on the evening tide. However, it took nearly two hours to get the vessel moored and by then the men had missed the best shopping hours of Christmas Eve. On my arrival aboard, Alfred Gibbs, the senior second officer, told me what had happened before the holiday, finishing with: "All normal as usual here, Eric!"

During the rest of the year I would learn the necessary seamanship to do the most interesting of all maritime jobs. What made it so pleasing to me was the fact the work was mainly in Cornwall and the Isles of Scilly. Our operations stretched westward from Trevose Head near Padstow, around the Islands to the Bishop Rock Lighthouse and then eastwards to the river Exe in Devon. This area covered the Eddystone, Wolf Rock, Longships, Round Island and Bishop Rock lighthouses and one lightship at the Seven Stones, all with lighthouse keepers and relief crew to be changed over. While the lighthouses at Godrevy in St. Ives Bay, St. Anthony Head and Plymouth breakwater needed routine work at times. The main rock lighthouses would be supplied with stores, while repair men also came to rectify faults. At times the ship carried Admirals, Government Ministers, Members of Parliament and the press to see our operations. We also had inspections by the superintendent Captain Harris (nicknamed Whiffy) and, of course, our bosses the Elder Brethren of Trinity House.

At Godrevy, Longships and Bishop Rock lighthouses we shared the work with local boatmen. In addition we would check all the stations in our area to see that their fog and light signals were in order, while 18 various buoys also needed servicing at regular intervals. A good deal of survey work was undertaken to ensure that the waters around Cornwall and Devon remained safe when wrecks and sinkings occurred.

My abiding memories of my first eighteen months as an officer on the THV *Stella* concerned two series of events which stretched out over a considerable time. Our most regular task during the year was to change half the crew on the Number 15 lightship, marking the Seven Stones Reef positioned some 12 miles off Land's End, every 14 days, then at the same time we changed the keepers on the rock lighthouses on a monthly schedule. These duties were subject to the weather, of course, and if the relief was delayed the time was wasted by both the keepers going on to the lighthouse and those coming off, because such time did not count for holidays or work. The relieving keepers would have to stay on the *Stella*, or very close by, in order to travel at short notice. The ship would normally wait in Mount's Bay if a failed attempt had already been made.

It was during the month of January that we had attended the Number 15 lightship and managed to effect the relief in a rising south-west gale, but on the way back to Penzance we were due to change one keeper on the Wolf Rock Lighthouse. This could only be done during a period of two hours on either side of low water, when the rock base was most exposed above the sea swirling around below.

The workboat had to attain a position with a rope from the stern to a small buoy at some distance from the rocks. Then approach the working position close to the Wolf Rock itself. Two ropes were then transferred to the base platform making it fast to the rock landing space. (In bad weather the whole operation could be very dangerous for everyone involved.) The keepers would rig a derrick on a mast structure and then swing it out over the boat. The keeper would strap himself into a harness and be swung on the derrick by hand up onto the landing platform. At this time the keepers handling the lift were in a hazardous position as the waves could sweep them into the sea, while the coxswain would have to be very much aware of swells swamping his boat. As the boat officer I was in charge, yet I relied on the coxswain's skill in this situation.

On this occasion, when we arrived at the lighthouse the ship waited some distance off the rock to observe the conditions. It was very quickly decided that no landing was possible and after a discussion with the senior keeper, Commander Parsons decided to return to Mount's Bay and anchor for the night.

Along with the keeper, half of us were allowed to have some hours ashore, returning at midnight to stand by for the next day's attempt.

At low water during the dark night, the keeper who was being relieved from the lighthouse reported that a landing was possible on that tide. Of course, because it was dark the crew were unable to do it at that time. Next morning, with all the crew on board, Commander Parsons informed us that even though the weather was no better we would have to return to the Wolf as the keeper had reported a possible landing during the night. It was not well received by the crew, who knew from years of experience on the Penzance Station that the conditions would be no better than the day before.

Needless to say, we steamed the thirteen miles out to the lighthouse, observed for nearly three hours, and returned to Penzance without the job being done. This tiresome routine was to be repeated for the next twenty-six days; the keeper reporting a landing was possible at night when we could not go and our returning the next day with no landing achievable. Although we found it possible to relieve the Seven Stones Lightship we were unable to get to the Wolf Rock. To say the crew of the *Stella* was near mutiny by this time would be an understatement. It had not only been the wind that had been the trouble but the swell, which continued to make a landing impossible even on a fine day. Finally, on the twenty-seventh day, the weather had marginally improved.

On this day the waves still made the boat surge, but the rock itself only had a light spray coming over the keepers as they worked. As soon as the boat was ready in position, the men on the rock rapidly swung the derrick to hoist the relief keeper, his gear and stores up to the lighthouse. Last of all the returning keeper and his gear were lowered towards the boat.

However, all did not go too well, and just as the man in the hoist was about to be lowered into the boat it moved astern and the keeper received a nasty ducking before being pulled aboard in a very wet and sorry condition.

As we were leaving, the soaked man moved past the coxswain in the covered area round the engine. At this point I heard the quiet warning given by Jimmy our coxswain to the very miserable keeper. "If you see more possible landings in the dark like you have in the last month you will drown next time!" I, of course, pretended not to hear the conversation.

That was the last time I saw that keeper in my Trinity service. It seemed that service on a rock lighthouse like the Wolf was not for him.

6

A New Commander
and Trouble in St. Ives Bay

During 1965 Commander Parsons left the ship and was transferred to Harwich. Low and behold Commander Tarrant now joined the *Stella* to take command. These were really happy days for me, Captain Harris retired as Superintendent and Captain Thompson replaced him at the Penzance depot. Commander Tarrant was a superb and talented captain of the ship and his new ideas for supplying stores made sure that we all had more time at home with our families. Remarkably he actually tied the *Stella,* by way of a ship's hawser line, to the Longships and Wolf Rock lighthouses using the ship's anchor and favourable tide conditions. This reduced the loading of stores, oil and water to less than half the time it had taken before, by pumping oil and water straight from the ship into the lighthouse tanks. A remarkable feat and as far as I know it had never been achieved before.

By January 1967 I had settled into a routine on the *Stella* based at Penzance; indeed life had never been so fulfilling. I had also an abiding wish to be involved in politics and had become the Chairman for the St. Ives Constituency Liberal Party. At the beginning of February 1967 I was nominated to fight an election for a seat on the St. Ives Borough Council. I had intended to campaign by knocking on doors at weekends and evenings occasionally when my duties allowed. It must have been very rare to have a full-time seaman actually wanting to be a councillor. However, it was not long before my efforts were to be badly affected by my work and the events in which the *Stella* was to be involved.

On Tuesday February the 14th *Stella* had embarked four lighthouse keepers, their gear and stores, and sailed from Penzance to effect the relief of the Seven Stones Light Vessel. As the superintendent was on leave at the time Commander Tarrant had relieved him at the depot and in command of the vessel was the Chief Officer, Bill Mathieson. Alfred Gibbs was acting 1st officer, myself acting as senior 2nd officer and a relief officer nick-named Geordie was acting as junior 2nd. The weather was quiet with a light south-westerly wind blowing and there was a moderate southerly swell, just enough to make the *Stella* move gently in the seaway. Shortly after midday the transfer of keepers, stores, water and oil had been completed. So by 3pm we were back and anchored outside Penzance harbour.

Above us high cloud was beginning to show itself in the sky, and the forecast was giving a twenty-four hour warning of a south-easterly gale for later next day. After the tasks of landing the returning lighthouse keepers and squaring up the ship, half of the crew were allowed to spend the night ashore. They were due to return to Penzance next morning at 8am. At that time a keeper was due to arrive to be placed on the Eddystone Lighthouse off Plymouth. Both Bill and Geordie stayed aboard and Alf and I went home for the night.

At 2am I was awakened from a deep sleep by the ringing of my telephone. It was the night watchman at the depot in Penzance. Due to rapidly deteriorating weather in Mount's Bay *Stella* had sailed from its anchorage and was coming to St. Ives Bay to pick up crew members on shore leave. At the time it seemed good news to me as I got an extra half hour in bed that morning.

So it was that we all gathered on the west pier in St. Ives harbour at eight the next morning. Out in St. Ives Bay there were by that time many vessels sheltering (by 10am there were 54 vessels at anchor). The storm was now exceeding gale force.

However, with some twenty or so crew on board, our workboat arrived back on board the *Stella* with little trouble. Little did I know at this point that in an hour and a half or so I would be in considerable danger in the same boat.

By 10am a message had arrived to say that our keeper for the Eddystone Lighthouse was on his way to the pier for the boat to bring him out to the ship. Now, of course, I was a candidate for the council election to come, and I was therefore a willing volunteer, dressed in my Trinity uniform, to take charge of the boat. Her crew consisted of Jimmy Quick as Coxswain, as well as two experienced sailors, Roger Symons and Nabo Nichols. All went well as we made our way into the harbour at St. Ives with the south-easterly storm helping the boat on its way. Alongside the west pier we waited for about twenty minutes for the keeper, Mr Harthill, to arrive. I spent the wait talking to my father-in-law and a couple of others on the pier itself. Then, after getting the keeper and his gear on board, we started our journey back to *Stella* waiting out in the anchorage a mile away.

Lulled by the experience of the best coxswain on the ship and the excellence of our boat I sat under the canopy of the engine as we left the safety of the port. As it happened, both Jimmy and myself were guilty of not noticing an approaching severe squall racing towards us with gusts of hurricane force wind within it. Quite suddenly it hit us and sea water poured into the boat over the bow and swamped the forward compartment. As the water flowed in at a tremendous rate the bow sank lower in the water and the stern rose, making the propeller less effective. In no time at all the craft became unmanageable, and was being swept by the tide and wind on to the rocks of the Island headland and certain destruction.

I made an immediate call to our ship for assistance and this brought the very fast launch of our second workboat to help us. However, on shore in the harbour area Mr James Perkin had noticed our predicament, and shouting to local shopkeeper, Mrs Cowlin, got her to phone 999.

Some minutes later our reserve boat with the junior second officer in command and Coxswain John Hall, came alongside us and began towing us clear of the rocks. But even so the tide and wind continued to sweep us all out to sea. At this point a helicopter from the Royal Naval Air Station at Culdrose arrived overhead, but luckily was not needed. By this time Acting Commander Mathieson had the *Stella* underway and we were a half mile clear of St. Ives head. There Bill manoeuvred the *Stella* between us and the breaking sea giving some protection. Then with some difficulty we managed to get the boat secured to the launching position alongside the ship.

With the use of a pump to clear the water we were able to lift the boat back on board, luckily in an undamaged condition. Then the ship returned to the anchorage amongst the other vessels in the bay.

Next morning the bad weather abated and we were soon on our way to Plymouth, arriving after dark that evening. In that time the better weather had faded and once more we were anchored in Plymouth Sound awaiting a chance to get out to the Eddystone Lighthouse.

We waited until the 17th of February before some fine weather gave us our chance to get to the lighthouse. But first Bill Mathieson, our commander, decided to do some routine maintenance on the Penlee Buoy at the western entrance to Plymouth Sound. This task meant that the ship went alongside the buoy and with the aid of her heavy working derrick lifted it on board, this way the gas bottles could be changed and the lamp serviced, the buoy itself painted and its mooring chain and sinker checked.

While this work was going on Bill stood on the wing of the bridge controlling the ship's engines and keeping it in the position of the buoy. As he was carrying out this vital work, he suffered a fatal heart attack and fell on the deck. I was working in the bridge at the time and, after summoning the acting Chief Officer, Alfred Gibbs, to take over the ship, I gave Bill mouth to mouth resuscitation (first pulling him clear of the ship's engine controls) for over half an hour in a vain attempt to help him.

While I struggled unsuccessfully with Bill, Alf got the ship away from the buoy and, on calling the port authorities, managed to get a berth to put the ship alongside in Plymouth. After another half hour alongside the jetty the paramedics gave up on Bill and we had to remain alongside. We were naturally devastated by these events.

Following this we had to clear up all the paperwork and await a relief commander. Typically in the next four days the weather stayed fine but we could not move, and as soon as the new chief, Commander Roberts, arrived aboard, the bad weather returned once more. So Mr Harthill still had not arrived on his station at the Eddystone Lighthouse and we were still waiting to get home.

At the end of the first week in Plymouth, the *St. Ives Times and Echo* printed the story of our drama in St. Ives Bay in lurid detail and stated that the incident happened because the boat's engine had failed. This, of course, was not true and our chief engineer Herbert was incensed and complained to me that the engine was still working when we recovered the boat. He intended to write a stiff letter to the newspaper pointing out its error. However, worried at what the publicity might do to my election chances, I managed to get Herbert to remain silent at this time.

Unfortunately, the following week the *St. Ives Times & Echo* reported the death of Bill and repeated the story of our engine failing in St. Ives Bay. Herbert was not to be denied this time and a stiff letter was sent to the editor despite my pleading.

However, as a politician, I was to learn that any publicity was good publicity and it did not affect my election prospects.

Another week passed and Commander Tarrant duly returned to the ship; and at last we carried out the relief. By then other reliefs were due at the Seven Stones Lightship and the Wolf Rock, while stores were urgently needed at the Longships Lighthouse. So it was that we did not berth in Penzance Dock until Friday the 17th of March, some 31 days after we had left our home port. That morning, after carrying out a night watch on board, little did I realise that the next month was to be much the same for a completely different reason.

7

The Wreck of the *Torrey Canyon*

18th March 1967 was hardly a routine day; much needed doing around the house and then there was the necessity to deal with bills and letters neglected following a month away from home. As it happened, I had not listened to any news broadcasts during the day, so it was a real bombshell of a surprise when the watchman at the Trinity House Depot at Penzance telephoned at 5pm to say that the *Stella* was sailing in two hours' time from the dock. I was ordered to return to the ship at once.

"Why?" I queried. "We've just been away for a month and I can't understand being called out again so quickly."

"There's a 100,000 ton tanker aground on the Seven Stones Reef called the *Torrey Canyon*, so you'd better get a move on," responded the watchman.

That really stunned me and, of course, after hurried preparations and a farewell to Jill and my two boys, I was on my motor scooter to return to the *Stella*.

On my arrival on board the crew were protesting to Commander Tarrant. Stores and food were needed before going back to sea, so surely we could wait until next day as nothing could be achieved in the hours of darkness.

Eventually the commander ignored his superintendent's order to proceed to the wreck site at once. Instead the ship was moved out of the dock and anchored off the port of Newlyn. There the

Co-Op store had to be especially opened to allow the ship's crew to obtain sufficient supplies to spend the next 36 hours at sea.

Then it was off to see the wreck which the whole world was talking about at that time – the SS *Torrey Canyon*. The huge vessel sat pinned to a large pinnacle of rock on the western side of the Seven Stones Reef called the Pollard Rock. This summit of an underwater hill in the reef had driven into the ship's hull like a spear. Every time the 974 foot long vessel moved with the slight westerly swell, the ship's steel plates would grind on the rock giving off an eerie scream like an animal in dire distress. All around the ship 100,000 tons of oil was seeping out into the blue sea turning it into a brown sludge. Carried on a westerly wind, the smell could be experienced 30 miles away on the mainland of Cornwall. As the *Stella* circled the wreck, planes carrying journalists shared the air space above with the regular helicopter flights going back and forth to the Isles of Scilly.

Also standing by the wreck was the Weissmuller salvage tug *Utrech*; while three other tugs were on their way to the scene from different ports. We, of course, checked out the lightship, put some stores on board, and received reports from the lightship crew. These were for our superintendent's information on the whole incident. After standing by for the day we went back to Penzance to refuel and load stores before returning to the wreck.

During this time helicopters were being used to place salvage personnel and pumps and other equipment on board the tanker. These men were under the control of a Captain H.B. Stal and were working to get the wreck's oil tanks airtight by sealing all parts of the deck open to fresh air. Then they had started to pump in compressed air to bring the tanker up in the water so that the vessel could clear the pinnacle of the Pollard Rock.

By Tuesday 21st March we had loaded our proper stores, and after a night at home, *Stella* was due to sail out of the Penzance wet dock at 1pm in the afternoon. Trinity House, in their wisdom, had ordered that we were allowed only two journalists with us. One represented the *Times* and the other a news agency. This caused a journalist 'demonstration' at our gangway, and about twenty or so press hounds all shouted for a right to sail with us.

At midday I received a message over our radio from the Seven Stones Lightship. The crew reported that an explosion had occurred in the engine room of the *Torrey Canyon* and that Captain H.B. Stal had been very badly hurt. This caused even more trouble, as the two journalists tried to get ashore to report the facts and the journalists on the quay got even more angry about not being able to get on board. By 1pm the problem had been solved, journalists ashore were not allowed on board, and those on board were not allowed ashore, and the ship was on its way.

On our arrival at the wreck we found out that two men had been blown into the water and that Captain Stal had died from his injuries. A few days' later the majority of the crew of the tanker were removed and *Stella* was to take part in the evacuation.

The Isles of Scilly Lifeboat *Guy & Clair Hunter*, under the command of Coxswain Matt Lethbridge, took off 23 members of the crew along with their gear and transferred them to the *Stella*. Matt and the crew then received some hot food and drinks from the *Stella*'s galley, while a mountain of suitcases and boxes containing everything from the ship's navigational clocks to bottles of spirits, cigarettes and so on were loaded on to the ship. In fact, we had noticed that when the lifeboat came alongside our vessel she was really low in the water with all the so-called crew's belongings on board.

We then proceeded to Penzance where the world's press were waiting. Our workboat (manned by the same crew who had got into trouble in St. Ives Bay more than a month before) landed the crew at the Lighthouse Pier.

Obviously all this was good publicity for me, a candidate standing for election to St. Ives Borough Council.

We waited at anchor in Mount's Bay as the four salvage tug crews, the salvage men, the captain and three officers of the tanker battled to tow the *Torrey Canyon* off the reef. In fact they did move the wreck just a small amount over the Easter weekend, but on Easter Sunday the weather began to take a turn for the worse. An approaching low pressure system produced a heavy swell and within hours the ship began to break up.

The salvors and remaining crew were taken off, and during this period a journalist with a TV cameraman got on board. Then people watching the TV report were able to hear the weird screaming sound as the ship's steel plates were giving way to the power of the sea. The reporter and cameraman did not stay long on the wreck which was a very wise decision.

Meanwhile, in Mount's Bay on Easter Monday, the superintendent arrived with orders for the *Stella*'s deployment.

With a south-west gale due, the ship was to leave the anchorage in the evening and tow the Seven Stones Light Vessel to Mount's Bay at first light next day. A difference of opinion then arose between the superintendent and our commander. The latter had protested that a south-westerly gale was already blowing and he could not be sure to move the light vessel in those conditions. Captain Thompson, a seasoned Trinity Officer, had already voiced this argument with the serving admiral in Plymouth. The Admiral had said that next day the wreck of the *Torrey Canyon* was to be bombed and the light vessel had to be removed from the area to avoid damage. The Admiralty would send a tug from Falmouth if *Stella* was unable to accomplish the task. Captain Thompson was adamant no tug would attempt the tow if Trinity House personnel said it could not be done.

The ship left Mount's Bay later in the evening in poor weather conditions, to proceed to the area of the wreck. At three o'clock that morning the gale moderated very rapidly and by daylight the conditions had improved considerably. Normally, to tow such a vessel, the crew of the *Stella* would connect its towline with the light vessel's anchor attached, and this would steady the light vessel while under tow. With the fine weather now getting better by the minute, Commander Tarrant ordered a ship's hawser to be made fast without the anchor. In a very short time the ship, with the Seven Stones Light Vessel under tow, was on its way back to Mount's Bay.

As *Stella* approached Land's End, an admiralty tug appeared coming from Falmouth. As the two vessels converged, the tug began signalling with a morse lamp (no VHF radios in those days).

The message stated: 'Are you happy with your tow and do you need assistance?'

Our reply was prompt: 'No thanks, all is well.'

The tug turned away and returned to Falmouth.

On arrival in Mount's Bay the crew of the lightship anchored their vessel and let go the tow rope. *Stella* then stood by awaiting further orders.

Captain Thompson arrived a quarter of an hour later in the very best of good humour. It seemed the Admiral in Plymouth had phoned him at 3am that morning to apologise for his remarks of the day before, stating, "Our tug has turned back for bad weather, you were right sir."

Captain Thompson had replied: "Our vessel *Stella* has not turned back and the light vessel will be removed at first light, Admiral. Now will you please let me get back to sleep."

One hour after our arrival the ship returned to the Longships Light House and began transferring stores for the keepers. All other vessels were being diverted from the wreck westwards around the Isles Of Scilly to avoid the area of the bombing. However, a few of the smaller coastal ships did pass close to the Longships Lighthouse away from the scene of the wreck.

As it was on a fine day we watched the attempts to destroy the *Torrey Canyon*, and to say the least, were not reassured at the failure to hit the target as one miss followed another. As it was, we were to observe the destruction of the rest of the wreck over the following weeks by the sea.

As the normal work load continued, every so often some important personages such as government ministers and even local councillors would come onboard to see the wreck for themselves. On one such occasion a whole crew of publicity men from the Royal Navy were present. During poor weather some of these non-seagoing people were violently seasick. *Stella*'s crew members were under strict orders not to embarrass them in their predicament.

8

Top of the Pole

During this time we were very aware of the continuing attempts to disperse the horrible clinging oil, left by the *Torrey Canyon*, from the picturesque Cornish coastline. So, of course, I was now to become particularly involved in this side of the story because I was standing as a Liberal candidate for the St. Ives Borough Council in an election to be held at the beginning of May 1967.

The local authorities in West Cornwall were small, and the two principle ones of St. Ives and Penzance covered the coast from St. Ives Bay around Land's End to Mount's Bay. From my home town of St. Ives a substantial fleet of various sized fishing boats were hired to spray the oil from the town all the way to Land's End.

The larger boats worked along the coast, while the smaller boats were tending the boom surrounding St. Ives Harbour and dealing with oil approaching the local beaches. Troops and council staff worked with heavy equipment ashore. Many of the coves to the west of St. Ives were not accessible by land and in these cases the workmen just rolled open drums over the clifftops causing major damage to the shell fishery of the area.

At the beginning of May I took 10 days leave and campaigned, amongst other things, to get a fair share of the clean-up work for small local boats engaged in tending the boom and other related tasks close to St. Ives. My efforts did have some success and partly as a result of this work, I was elected to the St. Ives Borough Council with 1123 votes, coming top of the poll of six candidates filling three seats.

There followed three years of very intensive politics in which I was to be involved in a number of disputes on the council. In some ways this affected my job on the *Stella*. I think it would take another book to relate it all, and although I was to have quite a lot of success, I never did feel at home in the world of politics.

In some ways I was unique as a serving sailor going to sea each week, having no scandal attached to my name and no business to protect in St. Ives. Very soon I found myself ranged against a very local establishment which was to do their best to bring me down over many years. However, I did, along with my other three liberal councillors, manage to open the completely secret committee meetings to the public. This allowed the electorate to find out beforehand what the council was going to decide, meaning they then would be able to object before any final decision was made at the full council meeting. It is a sad outcome, however, that in more recent years control of local planning, housing and services has passed to Cornwall Council at Truro, something which has caused considerable controversy.

Unfortunately this work was to bring me into conflict with Commander Tarrant. I was pretty sure that some of my critics got at him, and from this he began to show his dislike of my council work and to berate me in front of the crew. This treatment was very hard to take during my three years as a councillor.

In the five years I served with the Trinity House Lighthouse Service, I was to be involved in survey work, wreck disposal and many tasks carried out with boat work, the skills of which have been largely forgotten with the introduction of new technology. Promotion in the service was and is, I believe, by way of seniority, and this in my day entailed you serving in different parts of the country. In fact, by checking the retirements and resignations you could work out what your fate was going to be. By 1969 I had worked out that I would be forced to move to Harwich in Essex, which would obviously mean me leaving Cornwall. That for me was not acceptable, and so it was that I resigned from the prodigious service of Trinity House and began looking for a job locally.

9

Captain at Last

I soon discovered that the smaller of the two Isles of Scilly ferries needed a captain. So I visited the company's office in Penzance and had an interview with the managing director Henry Thomas, who then hired me for the job.

The *Queen of the Isles* had run aground in France with passengers on board and been stuck for 10 hours on a river bank, as well as having over twenty collisions with various quays over the last month of the season in 1969, so it seemed at the time I was very welcome with my certificate as a Master Mariner. It meant that after 15 years at sea I had finally gained the title of Captain Kemp. This new job meant that I did not stand again for the local council, and indeed I wasn't sorry to see the back of boring meetings in that particular august company.

The *Queen of the Isles* was launched in November 1964 by HRH The Duchess of Gloucester and had been running since 1965 between Penzance and the Isles of Scilly as well as to St. Ives and other charters. Among those charters were day trips to France and meeting sailors making Atlantic crossings from America, including Francis Chichester's famous voyage.

I joined the ship during the third week of January 1970, taking up the temporary position as Chief Officer under Captain John Ashford who was due to be promoted to company superintendent based at Hugh Town on St Mary's in the Isles of Scilly. While in dry dock for the first week I was largely left alone to get used to my new command and find my way around. The ship had been built at Charles Hill's Albion Yard in Bristol and because of a very cheap tender price was reputed to have been the main reason behind that company closing down. I now learned that the vessel had run at a loss for four years since arriving at Penzance and the future was uncertain. (I remain proud of the fact that in my year as captain a profit was made, but that's another story.) Overall the *Queen of the Isles* was 156 feet in length, had a beam of 30 feet and a draft of 10 feet when loaded. Her gross tonnage was 515 tons and, powered by 2 Ruston Hornsby Engines, her twin propellers gave her a speed of 15 knots. The vessel could carry 300 passengers and 80 tons of cargo.

My first visit to the bridge proved a revelation. The ship's navigational equipment was basic in the extreme, there being a magnetic compass to steer by as well as another compass on the deck above the wheelhouse. The company's pride and joy was the Decca Radar that had a poor 40 mile range but would give good results at 12 miles and less. Mr Thomas was of the opinion that the vessel would be able to keep perfect timing for the passengers with such a good navigational aid in fog! I spent over a half an hour searching for other equipment, such as an echo sounder (which gives the depth of water under the ship at any time), without success. There was only an old fashioned medium frequency radio in a small space at the rear of the bridge close to the chart table. My cabin, just behind the bridge, however, was spacious and comfortable and I was as keen as mustard to take over my new ship as soon as possible.

During the coming days I had to take two examinations to discover whether my knowledge of pilotage at Penzance and the Isles of Scilly was adequate enough to assume the responsibility of safeguarding the ship, crew and passengers. To be able to achieve this I had also to undertake a set number of trips to and from the Islands.

After finishing the refit I was to spend six weeks on the run between Penzance and St. Mary's. The passenger ship RMS *Scillonian*, being the senior vessel, spent six nights a week in

Penzance, this meant the *Queen of the Isles* spent those nights at St. Mary's. Due to this I did not see my wife and young family a great deal during this time. However, finally in March, I became the Captain of the *Queen of the Isles* with my own command.

The *Queen of the Isles* had a summer crew of 12 persons. My temporary Chief Office at the time was Sam Guy, an islander with extensive knowledge of the operating area. The chief engineer and 2nd engineer officers, John Allen and Robert Cray, were both local and very dependable. The bosun Harry Skewes always took the wheel on entering harbour or in difficult situations. The deck crew consisted of 4 seamen: Colin Downing, Colin Nichols, George McBurnie and John Le Breton. The catering crew consisted of Jerry the purser/steward and Wilfred the cook. A stewardess joined us later in the season when there were more passengers.

On that March morning the weather was calm and the sun rose to the south-east of St. Mary's showing the wonderful scenery of the islands at its very best, while the sparkling sea really invited a short cruise to Penzance. At St. Mary's the dockers loaded fourteen hundred boxes of flowers for the mainland while the crew prepared the ship for sea. I was up early to hear the BBC radio shipping forecast at 6.30am. My heart sank as the announcer predicted rain and increasing south-westerly wind for the forecast areas Plymouth, Lundy and Sole later in the day. We were scheduled to sail from St. Mary's at 9.30am and arrive at Penzance Lighthouse Pier at 12.15pm. Then departing from there at 4pm, the ship was due to arrive back at St. Mary's at 7pm, one and a half hours before low water.

On the previous evening we had moved the ship to the outer end of the pier to allow for the low water spring tide being so close to departure time. Alongside the end of the quay there was a narrow channel of slightly deeper water and this move ensured that we were not aground at the time of our leaving. Now, if there was a delay caused by bad weather, my problems in berthing the ship would be very much increased should the ship be late in returning. The low water then was just after 8.30pm, and at that time there would be very little water to get the ship alongside and

d

allow the passengers to disembark. This meant I had to try and hurry things along during the day if possible.

Just after 9.25 we had completed the loading of the cargo and some 15 passengers had come aboard. Our hatch was covered and we were ready to proceed when the bosun arrived on the bridge to take the wheel. His face was a picture of misery; and to say the least, I was alarmed at what could have gone wrong. Harry announced as he took up his position, "It's all going to be a disaster today."

"Why, what's happened?" I demanded.

" 'Cold Iron', we have a monk from Buckfast Abbey as a passenger, in all his robes, and it's bound to go wrong with a 'sky pilot' on board," he said gloomily.

So, of course, I smiled and dismissed his words with an loud, "Nonsense, old wives' tales, Harry," but I was a little worried as I backed the *Queen* off the quay and turned into the channel and worked our way out of the islands, passing the Bartholomew and Spanish Ledges Buoys as well as the Woolpack Beacon before setting our course for the Cornish mainland.

As it happened all went well at first, with a gentle south-west wind pushing us on, and we made excellent progress towards our destination. By noon we were approaching the Lighthouse Pier at Penzance and I was well pleased with our progress, even Harry seemed mollified as we came alongside and the discharge of the boxes of flowers began. The monk, together with the other passengers, shuffled away up the pier towards the town, his sandals slapping on the granite stones as he did so. By then I had conferred with the foreman docker Ben Green explaining the need to sail on time. He reassured me that there was not too much cargo to load and estimated that we would easily be on our way by 4pm. So with a light heart I left Sam, the chief officer, in charge and went home to St. Ives for a quick midday meal with my family.

On my way back to Penzance after a very pleasant meal, I noticed that the clouds were gathering and the wind was rising. To make it worse, on arrival at the Lighthouse Pier, I found that there had been a late rush of extra cargo and Ben Green was undoubtedly flustered. In answer to my question about being on time he replied:

"No way, Captain. You'll be late in sailing. In fact you will have to take some deck cargo as well, we will be filling the hold completely."

Sam was preparing the lashing for the cargo so I went down to the chief engineer to see if he would give me some extra speed.

"No way, Captain," he said. "We have one or two small problems and I do not recommend pushing the ship at the moment. After all, you wouldn't want the vessel to break down on her way over, would you?"

I had no answer to that one, so I made my way back to the bridge and looked with concern at the now worsening sea conditions in Mount's Bay.

At 3.50pm that afternoon things got even worse when Harry, with a really grim face, checked our monk back on board as a return passenger to the Islands.

With our cargo now on board and the 10 or so passengers warned of the bad weather to come, we left the pier. Then, as the wind increased to near gale force just before 5pm, and very shortly after passing the Low Lee Buoy near Mousehole, the ship began to pitch into the increasing sea with considerable violence. Already some of our passengers were suffering seasickness and things got worse as we struggled past the Runnel Stone buoy and out to the area of the Wolf Rock Lighthouse.

Just after 6.30pm a large container of petrol broke loose on the foredeck. This meant almost stopping the ship to ease the motion and give the chief officer Sam and the crew a chance of catching and restoring it to a safe position. So another 20 minutes were lost, and now, as I approached the Islands, it was pitch black with rain reducing the visibility, although fortunately the shelter of the land gave the ship some protection from the gale force south-west wind.

At Hugh Town, on St. Mary's, the company had arranged the leading lights to be on to help us to stay in the channel as we approached the quay.

It was now just 10 minutes after low water. My problem was

fairly simple, I had to approach the quay at a right angle, and turn into the deeper water without grounding on the bank less than a hundred feet away.

"It's that monk, he's 'Cold Iron'," said Harry as we approached the turn.

As the ship turned across the wind it became very difficult to manoeuvre, and sure enough the bow grounded on the bank as we missed the narrow channel entrance. As I battled to get the stern, which was still afloat, towards the quay, Colin Downing came to my aid and in the end proved Harry wrong in his gloomy predictions. Standing on the stern deck, his feet wide apart, he made a magnificent throw, with a heaving line attached to a mooring rope, across the gap onto the quay. Willing hands there soon pulled in the rope and made it fast on a bollard. This enabled me to get the stern very close to our berthing position. Before trying to get the bow afloat once more, we placed a gangway, stored on the quay, onto the stern deck and ushered the monk ashore with all dispatch, followed by his fellow passengers. Some 15 minutes later, and after quite a struggle, the ship had re-floated and moved alongside. It had been quite a day and yet we had arrived with our passengers and cargo in good order.

It was to be a good start to a busy year which was to end in disappointment. Over this period the *Queen of the Isles* was to be employed carrying cargo to the Islands with also a large number of passengers. During this time I quickly discovered that the community in Scilly was roughly divided into two groups. One group frequented the public houses (not my scene) and included the vast majority of the directors of the company. The other group consisted of chapel going Methodists. In actual fact, by marriage, I was distantly related to the Lethbridge family and therefore blessed into the second group. I would attend services with them on Sundays. I was a little concerned, though, that my not 'fitting in' with the directors of the shipping company was not liked and also that managing director, Henry Thomas, had been brought up in St. Ives alongside my father and still had a dislike of him.

10

Poorly Passengers and Passengers of Note

Soon it was Easter and my command started regular runs from Penzance to St. Ives and on to the Isles of Scilly. In between times, at my own suggestion, I was able to make short trips as far as Land's End and back to Penzance and these did make an extra profit for the company. On a voyage from St. Ives I was to experience two medical problems which in the end would be a lesson about different people's attitudes to illness. It was late in July and bookings of passengers were very heavy for all modes of transport to the Islands. As a result of this the *Scillonian* had a full complement of six hundred when leaving Penzance and the *Queen of the Isles* had a full total of three hundred on departure from St. Ives at the same time. As the *Scillonian* had cargo on board this meant that the *Queen of the Isles* must be first to berth in St. Mary's, and then pull off the quay to allow the larger ship to discharge during the day. So, making our best speed, I could just reach our destination first.

On this day the weather was fine but there was a fresh south-west wind and as usual the ship developed a lively motion as we proceeded toward the islands. As the vessel approached a point near Pendeen Light House, close to Land's End, the Steward, Jerry, arrived on the bridge. He informed me that we had a sick male passenger down in the saloon.

"We've got a problem, skipper," he told me. "I believe strongly that the man is suffering from seasickness but his wife says he has a condition which requires you to return to St. Ives and get him put ashore." With that Jerry produced a piece of paper with a word of eighteen letters that I could not even pronounce. "So what do I tell her, sir, are we going back?"

"No Jerry," I replied. "We would not be able to get alongside with the ebbing tide, and anyway, it's about the same distance to St. Mary's. I will come down and have a look at him."

So a few minutes later I viewed a very seasick man who was extremely miserable. Neither of the couple were happy at my explanation that we would be proceeding. In order to reassure them, I explained that I would speak to the port health doctor in Penzance and, if it was necessary, ask the Sennen Cove Lifeboat to meet us and take him off the ship.

Back on the bridge I made a telephone call to Doctor Leslie in Penzance. I spelt out the eighteen letter word as it was written in front of me. Doctor Leslie was a doctor of the old school who did not mince his words.

"Stuff and nonsense, Eric, this condition is not affected by seasickness. However, I will have the ambulance on the quay at Scilly for your arrival and we will take him up to the hospital and, if my instincts are correct, keep him there for a while to teach him a lesson. I predict that as you reach the shelter of the Islands you will find he will recover very rapidly. Just the same, this action will cover both of us if there is any comeback."

In fact the doctor was absolutely correct, and as we approached the channel between St. Agnes and St. Marys our patient was on deck enjoying the sights and, according to one of my crew, saying he was hungry.

When we had tied up alongside at Hugh Town I had positioned myself at the gangway. Sure enough the fourth passenger to disembark, smiling all over his face, was our sick passenger.

"Excuse me, sir," I said, "the ambulance is waiting to take you up to the island hospital for a checkup. We need to reassure ourselves that you are OK."

I then led him down the gangway protesting that he was well.

His protests were of no avail and he was soon on his way with his wife for a long delay, cutting short his visit to the islands.

By this time Henry Thomas was on the quay and urging me to get the ship out to an anchorage to let the *Scillonian* come alongside. But as I returned to the bridge Jerry turned up with a very worried look on his face.

"Captain, we have another passenger in the forward saloon and I am sure he has had a bad heart attack but nobody has informed us of the trouble."

The ambulance had gone, the staff on the quay under the direction of Henry Thomas was casting off the lines and my shouts for a delay were ignored. So I anchored the ship very close to the quay, clear of the *Scillonian,* and we then placed the poor man in a stretcher and launched the ship's lifeboat to get him ashore. We were to learn he had suffered a serious heart attack and was immediately air-lifted to the mainland for treatment. That was a serious lesson for any master of a ship; always be ready for the unexpected. Thankfully in the end the man did recover and all turned out well.

During the summer I was lucky to have some very interesting passengers. Early in the year the Cornish poet Arthur Caddick brought his wife and son on board, and insisted on taking a very exposed position on deck near to the bridge.

To say the least, the weather was boisterous and the *Queen* was rolling and pitching quite violently as we proceeded in a strong north-westerly wind along the coast from St. Ives.

Convinced that Arthur would soon see the error of his ways, I told the chief officer Sandy Wilson to keep an eye on him and assist when the family wanted to move.

Sandy became worried when Arthur produced a flask of whisky from his pocket. It was indeed fortunate that I could see what was happening from my position in the wheelhouse. As Sandy attempted to reason with the poet he stood up, clearly affected by the amount of whisky he had already imbibed, and fell against the ship's side rails. The ship had rolled heavily to a large wave pounding its side. Both Sandy and Arthur's son also slipped trying to help him, and it was only after I joined them that we got him back into a place of comparative safety.

In actual fact Sandy had been a policeman so was good in such situations, which was as well as we had to forcibly remove the family to a lower inside saloon for their own safety. After that little drama I always kept one of my sailors on deck while carrying passengers, to ensure their safety whatever the weather.

Mr Ray Gunter MP was another passenger on the *Queen*. At that time he was Minister for Labour Relations and the Trade Unions in the Harold Wilson Government. He preferred our ship so that he could keep his distance from Harold who often travelled on the larger *Scillonian*. His tales of Barbara Castle and others were most interesting as we travelled between the islands and the mainland.

Yet another who travelled with us, to see the start of the tall ships' race in 1970, was Frank Gibson, and he took a wonderful picture of the *Sagres*, the winner of this particular race to Portugal, and presented me with a copy. I produce it in this book with the permission of his daughter.

However, it was one more passenger who travelled with us who really caused me the most professional satisfaction. In the week before the summer Bank Holiday, Commander Tarrant attempted to travel to Scilly by the helicopter, only to be told that there were no seats available. Disappointed he applied to the company office for a ticket on the *Scillonian*, only to be given the same news that the tickets had all been allocated. "But," said the booking clerk, "I can get you a passage on the *Queen of the Isles*," and in the end, treated just like any other passenger on board, he did travel with his former shipmate to St. Mary's.

11

Mersey Docks & Harbour Board Go Bust

Towards the end of the summer the *Queen of the Isles* was to carry out two charters of some note. The first was from Torquay when over one weekend the ship made two trips to the Channel Island of Guernsey and both were very successful with full loads of passengers. The second was to the Port of Liverpool and we were chartered to the port authority. There they allocated us a berth on the Liverpool Landing Stage overlooked by the famous Liver Birds on the port waterfront building. As sheer luck would have it, the lock gate men, who controlled all access to the Liverpool Cargo working docks, went on strike on the Sunday before our trips began.

On the Monday morning a massive amount of alcohol and food was delivered to the ship, along with special waiters and other staff. Then at 11am various representatives of all the main shipping companies, export and import companies, as well as Members of Parliament, boarded and were made welcome by representatives of the Port Authority with drinks etc. Special passengers were entertained in the captain's cabin, without me, of course. I was busy shifting the ship out into the river, where anchored, our passengers leisurely dined with the best of food in the saloon.

After lunch we proceeded up river to the entrance to the

Manchester Ship Canal before turning around and steaming out to the light vessel at the entrance to the River Mersey. After stopping briefly alongside the lightship and letting the passengers on board for a look around, we proceeded back to the landing stage and the end of our little jolly for the day.

Of course, even by the first day, ships were anchoring to await the end of the strike going on at the docks. By the third day the queue had grown to about twenty ships and even more by the weekend. This farce ended on the Saturday when, with the press on board, a rather tipsy Chairman of the Port Authority sat at a table on the afterdeck of the ship trying to explain why the authority had been declared bankrupt, and why he had chartered the *Queen of the Isles* for a substantial fee while his authority was broke. Ah well, all in a captain's day, I suppose? We then had a couple of trips from Fleetwood to the Isle of Man, before returning home to Penzance – only to find out that the *Queen of the Isles* was for sale!

As it happened at this time Captain Davies, the master of the *Scillonian*, had died and I assumed wrongly that I would be replacing him. So I was both surprised not to be told of the sale of my command, and also when an advert appeared in the local paper for a captain of the *Scillonian*. Of course I applied, and I then found out I was not even on the shortlist for the job. However, I was in for one last event which just showed how unreasonable the company could be.

We had just sailed to St. Ives for our penultimate voyage of the season, and when the ship berthed in the harbour I could see very high cloud coming in from the west. On listening to the forecast I realised that bad weather was definitely on the way. Already there was a movement of swell in the bay, and I asked Captain John Thomas, the St Ives agent (brother of Henry Thomas):

"How many passengers tomorrow, John?"

"Seventy, at least," he replied.

"Well," I said, "you had better give them their money back. The *Queen* will not be here because of the weather."

He replied by referring me to his brother and believed I would not be allowed to cancel the forthcoming trip.

By coincidence a Captain Thomas (no relation to the managing director) had been appointed to the *Scillonian*, and on my arrival back at Penzance his ship was on the Lighthouse Pier and ready to load early next morning. I berthed the *Queen* on the Albert Pier. This meant that for my ship to sail from Penzance with the tides as they were, I would have to sail from there out into the bay and replace the *Scillonian* after it had sailed.

By six o'clock the next morning a full south-west gale was blowing and the forecast predicted that it was going to increase to storm force. I phoned Henry Thomas in Scilly. He sounded grumpy and demanded to know what I wanted. I informed him that due to the extreme weather I would not be sailing for St. Ives. He got very angry and, in the end, I offered to put the ship out in the bay, but told him he would need another captain to take her to St. Ives. He hung up on me and all I could do was to tell the crew we were not going and put them on routine cleaning duties.

By nine o'clock the sea was breaking over the Lighthouse Pier and yet the *Scillonian* was still loading deck cargo, albeit with great difficulty. Dodging the spray, I walked around to the ferry and warned the captain of the difficulties he was facing. His reply stunned me.

"Mr Thomas says I must go. I have thirty passengers booked and a full load of cargo. I have refused to take a car but I do have deck cargo."

All I could do was to shake my head and return to my own ship to await developments.

Mid-morning, and with the *Queen* high and dry in her berth and clear of the now raging storm, I turned on the ship's medium frequency radio to listen to events out in the south-west approaches. Every twenty minutes Land's End Radio was calling the *Scillonian* and not getting a reply, so at midday I made my way to the company office to ask what was happening.

"We are not talking to you," they informed me. "You did not proceed on your trip today as ordered."

I got up a bit tight and in the end the clerk did admit that they did not know where the *Scillonian* was.

I made my way back to my ship and by two o'clock in the

afternoon the authorities were broadcasting messages asking if any ship had see the *Scillonian*. Shortly after two o'clock the Wolf Rock Lighthouse reported spray going right over the tower some 120 feet above the sea. The keeper said he could see a vessel almost lost in the murk and he could tell it was white in colour and about a mile north of him. He estimated that some of the gusts of wind were getting close to one hundred knots.

About a quarter of an hour later a very faint voice was heard. It was the *Scillonian* calling Land's End radio. The master reported that the radio aerials had been damaged, that three of the passengers had been hurt and there was loss and damage to the cargo. Captain Thomas asked to speak to Henry Thomas but he was not available and Captain Ashford then came on the line. I could not believe my ears at the conversation, it went like this:

"Please can I return to Penzance. The ship is making no way in this storm and we have passengers who have suffered injury?"

Superintendent John Ashford was direct and to the point: "You have a decision to make, Captain. If you get to Scilly, conditions here are so bad you would have to anchor until the storm has past. Or you can return to Penzance. I leave it to you," and with that he terminated the call.

Some three quarters of an hour later the *Scillonian* came into Penzance and an ambulance took the three passengers away with minor injuries. Added to this there were all sorts of people examining their cargo and making claims for items damaged through seawater getting into the hold.

Next day the company officials would not speak to me because I did not go, and would not speak to Captain Thomas because he did go.

By Monday they were speaking again, but these events left a bitter taste in my mouth. Three weeks later I found out through a television news item that the *Queen of the Isles* had been sold.

The company was to offer me the chief officer's job on the *Scillonian* but I refused and spent six weeks standing by my first command at Penzance until the *Queen* was taken over by her new owners.

12

Self-Employment

A new era was about to begin, but it was not immediately evident to me how things would work out. For the first few weeks leading towards Christmas 1970 I was on the dole and I certainly did not enjoy it. I had been on wages of seventy pounds a week and now we were short of money and Jill my wife, while still looking after our two small children, decided to take in bed and breakfast customers.

There seemed no jobs that I fancied coast-wise at the time, but my opportunity came when an advert appeared in the local paper for a Trinity House Pilot for the port of Penzance. I had little difficulty getting the job, as I already held a pilotage licence for the port and the Pilotage Committee was chaired by Captain Parsons of *Stella* fame by this time. He had actually been given the job as Inspector of the South West Trinity Lights and Navigation Marks and was back living locally.

What I was to discover was that I would be one of the very poorest Trinity House Pilots in England and Wales. The job was one of self-employment and the rates of pilotage were fixed at a very low rate. I was only responsible for Penzance as there were two other pilots engaged in the port of Newlyn where there was a good trade of stone to various ports in southern England and the near continent. They had a splendid pilot boat which did a good deal of work on passing ships in the bay. I was also expected to buy my own pilot boat and employ a boatman, even given my slender means.

In order to get me started the local dry dock was willing to employ me as a rigger and let me use their Tug *Primrose* to assist in my work as a pilot. In actual fact, this very small memorable vessel did look something like a tug above the waterline. However, below the waterline in looked more like a bathtub. When I had hired my boatman Leo Downing, a quite extraordinary character, on a self-employed basis, we ventured out into the bay with it to test the very good references the dry dock manager had given it.

At the time there was some swell in the bay and Leo, who had experience of the so-called vessel, warned me of what would happen. *Primrose* ascended the first wave and, without any change on the steering, turned right round and headed back to Penzance! Efforts to reverse the process only resulted in the vessel heading towards the nearby rocks. Indeed, our efforts to get the tug back to harbour took quite some time and left me very shaken.

There followed a rather bad tempered conversation with the dock manager Jimmy Rowe, in which I had to say that I was very sorry but I was not willing to risk my neck going outside the harbour in such a craft. Jimmy answered with his almost stock answer to any pilotage problem: "Hard luck. That's all you can expect. It's up to you how you get aboard. Just the same, I expect you to get the ships in and out of the harbour without delay."

As it happened I was able to negotiate with the other two Newlyn pilots, Leslie Davis and Ian Wilson, to have their pilot boat do the task – at a cost, of course, which left me still depending on my wife's efforts of bed and breakfast. On a week of no ships I could, with overtime, make about forty pounds, but even on weeks when I was busy, the return from the dry dock company was still very small indeed.

It seems incredible now but the first vessel I piloted at Penzance was the MV *Henrietta H*, a German coaster carrying 500 tons of fertiliser for local farmers. I managed to dock the vessel in the wet dock and sail the ship again twenty-four hours later. I boarded the vessel in the bay with the help of Ian Wilson using the pilot boat *Medway* (a boat which I would own myself in future years). The whole operation netted me ten pounds and nine shillings out of which I paid the boatman three pounds, and Trinity house took part of the fee for my pension rights.

Over the months of January and February I was to assist twenty vessels. These included the large dredger *Hoveringham I*, in for dry docking and the largest vessel during my time there to use the port, and certainly one of the largest ever to get into the wet dock. There was also the brand new *Esso Penzance*, at 340 feet long with a beam of 48 feet, only just making it through the narrow entrance of 50 feet width. This vessel was on a courtesy visit and the only berth long enough for the ship's length was the west wall. We also had well known and familiar names from that time such as the MV *Warwickbrook*, MV *Cambrian Coast*, *Michael M*, and *Commodore Goodwill*, to name but a few. Without my own pilot boat I only received £160 for all this work and it was obvious to me that I had to buy a pilot boat as soon as possible.

Such an opportunity came my way at the beginning of March when a 23 foot open crabbing fishing boat came on the market at Cadgwith Cove just east of the Lizard. In fact, I was already aware of the tragic circumstances which forced the sale of this trim little craft called the *Grey Ling*. Her owner had been out fishing in the Lizard area with his teenage son, and while placing his crab pots on the fishing ground the father had his legs entangled in the ropes connecting the pots. His son, only a young man, had tried to help his father by cutting the ropes but did so in the wrong place causing the heavy gear to drag the man overboard to his death by drowning. Now the boat was to be sold at auction some seven months after this tragedy.

I had just £200 to spare in our bank account and was able to raise a lone on my account for a further £600. I gave the money to my father, who went to the auction in his most expensive clothes and looking the part of a rich man. I never showed any interest and stayed away from the auction, therefore letting the bidders think they were up against my dad. The auctioneer opened the bidding at £600 and then asked if anyone else would bid. Dad then, in his best commanding voice, bid £800 and a silence fell over the whole assembly. No further bid was forthcoming and so I obtained my first boat.

As it turned out the seven weeks following the sale were very frustrating. I quite naturally wanted to get *Grey Ling* back to Penzance to earn some money. However, with working all week and having to pilot a number of ships, I could only bring the boat over during a weekend, and every time I tried a gale of wind managed to force me to cancel the voyage.

On one Friday evening, in rough southerly weather, we managed to get a tanker, the *Pass of Glenogle*, into the dock just as the weather was rapidly getting worse. The captain of the ship was very grateful to be in a safe harbour as the wind rose to gale force outside. As Leo my boatman and I sat in his cabin, this mariner from the north of Scotland produced a bottle of whisky to celebrate. Because I was driving (I owned a three-wheeler van at the time) and a Methodist local preacher, I declined. Leo, however, accepted and the two settled down to a bit of a party.

By now I was desperate to get the *Grey Ling* to Penzance and as usual I had my father on standby to crew with Leo and myself should we get an opportunity to shift my boat on the following day, Saturday.

As it happened, Leo was convinced that he was a hard drinker but he had found his match in the captain of the *Pass of Glenogle*. By the early hours of that Saturday morning Leo had staggered back to his home and relapsed into a deep sleep while the ship's captain was still enjoying his second bottle of whisky.

At daylight that morning the gale was still blowing from the south-west making for very rough weather at the Lizard Point which we would have to pass to get to Penzance. But then I noticed that the barometer was rising and I was sure that the wind was soon to shift to the north-west and bring an immediate improvement to conditions at the Lizard Point. As previously planned I called up my father, a master mariner like myself, to help me crew the boat from Cadgwith to Penzance, and organised that my father-in-law, a garage and taxi owner, would take us to

Penzance and collect Leo before travelling to the cove at Cadgwith.

On arrival at my boatman's rented rooms we found Leo suffering from a hangover and unwilling to countenance a voyage around the Lizard Point to Mount's Bay. After a little while arguing, I was able to persuade Leo that we could carry out trials to the east of the Lizard where the conditions were sheltered.

The *Grey Ling* had been stored in a shed close to the village and to get the boat to sea I had to pay a number of volunteers a total of £20, from my limited resources, to pull the boat down the road and launch her into the sheltered waters of the cove. Leo was busy checking the engine and fuel and did not notice me slipping away to a phone box to warn the coastguard that we were sailing to Penzance. The coastguard's comment on my plans was hardly reassuring, "I suppose I cannot persuade you to delay for a day or so?"

The answer was emphatic: "No, needs must!"

I could see that the members of the launching gang were in high spirits when I got back. My father had heard them talking and congratulating themselves on another anticipated £20 when we returned and they helped to get the boat back to the shed.

"We'll see. . ." I said grimly.

So just after midday we set out from Cadgwith. At first all went well, and shortly after we started out the cloud started clearing and the wind changed direction to the north-west, reducing almost at once the heavy seas running around the Lizard Point. In the meantime I had directed the boat towards the point while Leo concentrated on the engine, checking to see if it was overheating. By the time he looked up Cadgwith was well astern and we were approaching the tide race and rough sea off Cornwall's southernmost point. My boatman's reaction was one of fury to say the least.

"What are you doing?" he fumed as I tried to explain that I had just got to get the boat back to Penzance to earn some money to pay us a decent living. My dad tried to explain also and suffered a real mouthful of swearing from Leo.

However we were now committed, and *Grey Ling*, a boat built in Porthleven close to the Lizard, rose to the waves in a really impressive way. There was no doubt that she was a superbly built cove boat and in her element as the spray from her bow soaked the three of us. By the time we had reached our destination we looked like snowmen due to the salt water spray.

It was indeed a very rough trip as we rounded the Lizard Point and gradually moved into the calmer waters of Mount's Bay. We eventually arrived in Penzance for the early evening tide and passed in through the gates to a secure berth in the wet dock. We had pushed the *Grey Ling* very hard and it proved necessary to lift the boat up onto the quay and repair the hull to stop all the leaks which had developed on the way. Leo, of course, did those repairs for me. Later I was to hear him boasting how well the *Grey Ling* had made the trip and that he had complete faith in the boat. I was also to find out that the coastguards had watched us all the way from Cadgwith to Penzance from their clifftop lookouts, concerned about our safety.

Leo Downing proved to be a really interesting and, most of the time, a very valuable boatman. I could not afford to employ him full-time and he worked as a self-employed man for me. He was a very good carpenter and had served in the army, being present at the invasion of Egypt in 1956, serving in a boat squadron. He had, as far as I know, six brothers, all of whom were Methodists and more than one of them worked in their father's undertaker's business. But Leo liked his pint, swore like a trooper and was a real loaner. His family had long disowned him and he often complained that they had tricked him out of his inheritance when his mother died. He had been working with me about four months when a really amusing incident occurred.

At the time we were waiting in Penzance for the arrival of a regular visitor: the MV *Worcesterbrook* with 1500 tons of household coal destined for the local coal merchants J.H. Bennetts. Leo was normally a very talkative man but on this particular evening he was quiet and in a poor temper. After some time he admitted to me that he was about to be evicted from his single room lodgings. I was, of course, concerned as he was a very loyal worker.

However, as with everything to do with Leo, it was a complicated story. He lived in an old rambling house of considerable size not far from the centre of Penzance town and also near the harbour. He was a sub-tenant to the man who rented the building and he paid his rent to him. He had a rent book but paid the rent to the tenant by carrying out maintenance on the building and acting as a caretaker of sorts. In the previous year to Leo's employment with me the tenant had died. Leo had saved his rent but nobody had come to collect it. Now, after a year, he was summoned to court with an eviction order for nonpayment of rent.

I did my best to help him and paid for a solicitor from Newquay to come and represent his interests. In court, at St. John's Hall in Penzance, the judge ruled against Leo and gave him six weeks to vacate the property. In the court building, before the hearing, my boatman had been in deep conversation with a little old lady who owned another similar property right on the waterfront in Penzance. In the case following Leo's, she appealed for possession of one of her single room lets and won. Following this Leo was to inform me that all was well and he would teach the man who had evicted him a lesson he would not forget.

Over the next six weeks he removed his tools and meagre possessions to his new digs on the seafront. Then he proceeded to place strong new locks on the door and windows of the old digs. In the room was a heavy old-fashioned bedstead, a large oak stained table, a stained old carpet, a rocking chair, window curtains, bedding and some much used and stained crockery.

On the day of eviction Leo was to play his favourite game of disappearing; but at the same time watching the bailiff looking for him. I must admit I'd spend hours looking for him when he felt aggrieved about anything and he would only appear just as the ship was about to arrive or sail. Now he was playing the game in deadly earnest to annoy his enemy the bailiff. That poor man had spent the whole morning and early afternoon being told by various people that they had seen Leo about a half an hour before.

By 1.30pm in the afternoon Leo was installed in the next door house in a room overlooking the garden of his digs. Promptly at

2pm the bailiff, accompanied by a policeman and a carpenter, arrived at the house. With great difficulty they broke into the room and so began the really tiring job of dumping all the furniture on the lawn. By 4pm the bailiff and his party were surveying the results of their hard work, with all the furniture and contents in the garden. At that point, prompted by Leo, his friendly neighbour looked over the fence and asked the policeman what they were doing.

"Removing Mr Leo Downing's possessions," replied the policeman. "If you see him will you tell him to remove them from the garden, please."

"They're not his," the neighbour replied. "They belong to the man who died a year ago."

After a short silence there was a conference between the carpenter and the policeman. Shortly afterwards they both left, telling the bailiff that their working day had come to an end and so leaving him to cope alone. I don't know how the bailiff managed but I can well remember Leo's satisfaction at the outcome.

13

A Resignation and a
Wreck in Penzance Harbour

During my first year as the Penzance Pilot I was to have quite a struggle to keep the pilotage running due to my lack of resources. Over all it could be said I had done well. Acting on my own as pilot I was, during the first twelve months, to pilot 96 British registered and 50 foreign registered vessels in and out of the port as well as shifting them in and out of the dry-dock and round the various berths in the harbour. If it had not been for the extra wages I earned at the Holman Dry Dock it would not have been possible to meet my commitments. Equipment, as well as paying wages, fees and maintenance all took their toll on my strained bank balance. However, with the addition of my wife's income as a local schoolteacher and her bed and breakfast guests, we did survive and my position improved as the months wore on. Although, by the end of the year, I had still not managed to fit my boat out with pilotage lights and had to make do with a torch to flash at approaching vessels so that they could see us coming.

By December 1971 my relations with the Holman Dry Dock and its manager Mr Jimmy Rowe had reached a difficult stage. It was natural that the needs and wishes of the Dry Dock Company should at times be different to those of the Trinity House pilot. At times the Dry Dock Company was under much pressure to shift ships in and out of the dock, which was controlled by the depth of water caused by different tides during the month. As the pilot I was charged with advising the captains of these same ships on the weather and its effect on the safety of the vessel. During my first year there had been quite a few minor accidents to vessels caused by the pressure put on both the captains and myself as an employee of the company. I was to learn that agreeing to take chances was to my detriment.

If all went well nothing would be said, but if any ship moving in high wind conditions made heavy contact with a quay I was always blamed. During my first year some six ships faced this situation and I had to answer to my pilotage commissioners for these events. Often I had warned captains of the dangers but they had been under pressure both from the dry dock company and their owners who wanted the repairs done as quickly as possible. During the year Holman's had pacified the ship owners by making repairs to any damage done on these occasions. Things came to a head three weeks before Christmas when a small Coastal Tanker, the *Esso Brixham,* had difficulty in making some repairs. The vessel had been in the dry dock twice as well as being moved several times over a stay of three weeks.

No damage had been done to the ship during this time but for the first time in my pilotage career in Penzance, a single bill came to over £200. Mr Jimmy Rowe took a violent exception to a mere pilot charging such a fee and refused to pay. Of course, I had one advantage – having a monopoly of the pilotage for the port. So when confronted with this problem, I made a verbal protest in Holman's office. Present at the time was the superintendent for the next vessel to dry dock, the MV *Yewmount.* I informed the deputy manager, Mr Graham Brigdon, that the next ship would not get a pilot if I was not paid. There followed a confrontation with Mr Holman himself in the boardroom and much to his disgust Jimmy, as he was known, had to pay up. As it happened, two weeks later I received a letter from the company, copied to ship owners, saying that all ships coming to Penzance of less than 1500 tons gross tonnage did not have to use the services of a pilot and Holman's would no longer pay for these charges in any contract repair.

Four days before Christmas the Irish cargo vessel *Mossville*, 547 gross tons, arrived in Mount's Bay to dry dock over the seasonal holiday. Approaching Penzance her master was aware he was late for the tide and hurrying to get into the port. Penzance entrance has a set of rocks just outside which is marked by a steel pole with a round steel basket on its top standing out from the water at high tide. However, in those days it had no identification light for night time navigation.

As Leo and I came around the pier into the bay in our pilot boat *Grey Ling* we could see that the coaster *Mossville* was heading straight for these rocks. We had no radio or lights at this time, so we could not warn the captain of this danger. All we could do was to get to him as fast as we could.

Fortunately I arrived on board just seconds before disaster. As I climbed the ladder I ordered the captain to alter course by screaming, "Hard a Starboard NOW." I arrived on the bridge with the ship now changing its heading, then I ordered the ship's wheel put hard the other way to port, checking the swing and now taking the stern away from the rocks. When the danger had passed I pointed out to the grateful master just how close he had come to being on a shipwreck.

After we had docked the vessel in Penzance I stayed with the captain to have a well earned cup of tea. As we sat talking, the deputy manager of the dry dock arrived to tell the captain that he need not use my services to shift the ship into the dry dock. It was a moment of quiet satisfaction for me. The master now stood up to his full height and informed Mr Brigdon that *he* decided when he had a pilot not the dry dock, as well as praising me at the same time. Needless to say, Graham Brigdon disappeared out of the cabin rather rapidly with little to say.

Following this incident I gave my notice to Holman's and became a full time pilot. Now I was the master of my own destiny even if I still had to battle with the dry dock management from time to time. It was of note that Holman's were to accuse me of recklessness on a number of occasions. The first time was following this incident and named every problem I had in the previous year. It was a matter of pride with me that I was cleared of all blame in five of the cases and highly praised for my efforts in the sixth occasion. These events were to be rather common, and disputes about boat assistance were to continue throughout my time as a pilot in Mount's Bay.

There were times when other events proved quite dramatic. and the story of the visit of the MV *Yewhill* (1500 gross tons) to Penzance in March 1974 was notable by any standards. It was the time when I first became aware of much increased wind speeds in the storms that year.

I was contacted in the third week of the month by the agent Del Johnson from J.H. Bennetts Ltd acting for the ship. At the time a severe southerly gale, typical for that time of year, had caused the port of Penzance to have the dock gates locked with two wooden booms preventing all movement into and out of the inner harbour. As the gale had been well forecast, on my orders Leo my boatman placed the pilot boat *Greyling* inside the dock. Outside the boom gates the *Scillonian* was moored on a tidal berth with some shelter from the storm, and the other two outside berths, the Lighthouse Pier and the north arm, were empty due to the weather.

The sea was already very turbulent and the swells were breaking over the Lighthouse Pier wall, with the spray blowing across the whole dock area as I was talking to the agent on the phone. Del was to tell me that the *Yewhill* had serious water leaks in the engine and various other damage caused by the weather in the Bay of Biscay. The vessel was making slow speed towards Penzance and was hoping to dock for emergency repairs. I admitted to Del that there was little I could do as my pilot boat was trapped in the closed wet dock. He insisted I help in some way as the ship could not remain in the bay and must be berthed somewhere. I agreed to be in Penzance the next morning on her arrival and if possible to board the ship with the Newlyn Pilot boat which, of course, I did not own.

So at eight the next morning I arrived at Newlyn harbour across the bay to see if I could achieve something. In one respect the situation had improved as the wind had now shifted in a

These are the three children from *Rosalind* who were
rescued together with four adults.

Eric with the Irishman leaving the
lifeboat following his rescue.

Leo Downing in the pilot boat *Vestal*,
Mount's Bay.

Miss Tita.

Lightship under tow of pilot boats.

Eric meets Her Majesty The Queen.

Eric talking to the Duke of Kent on his visit to St. Ives.

Eric introducing the Duke of Kent to the deputy launching
authorities: Lt Commander Jack Rowe and Captain
Denis Proudfoot, and also Coxswain Tommy Cocking.

Stores on the pilot boat *Medway* for the
tug *Fairplay X*, Mount's Bay, 1980.

Tug *Fairplay X* in Mount's Bay at sunrise.

Lady Bird wreck. The helicopter hovers over the
mast which is all that remains visible.

Coaster discharging house coal at Penzance, 1982.

Dredger *Pop Eye* aground in St. Ives Bay.

south-westerly direction. This had made conditions for an approach to Penzance possible, although still difficult because the vessel was having problems with the engine. However, the sea conditions meant that the gates remained closed to the wet dock, and the only safe berth outside was occupied by the passenger ferry *Scillonian II*.

At 8.45am I got on board the *Yewhill* in the bay and much to my surprise, as I conferred with the captain, the *Scillonian* emerged from the Albert Pier bound for the Isles of Scilly. This allowed me to use that berth as the ferry was not due back until next day.

"It's only a temporary solution to our problems, Captain, but by then we might have an improvement in the weather. I hope so anyway," I said.

The captain agreed, and with that certain amount of luck all pilots in Penzance need without assistance, we berthed satisfactorily close to the railway station and the very large car park which at one time had been a part of the harbour.

As I left the ship I tried to impress the captain and chief officer of their vulnerable position on this particular pier. By then a weather forecast had predicted a southerly storm with winds over 80 knots in strength. Already the water level where we were was some two feet higher than usual. My advice had been to put all the best ropes and wires out to tie the ship to the pier and to have his crew stand by these moorings during the evening's high tide when the vessel would float once more. As it was, the captain was still celebrating escaping the last stormy blast and sadly for him he ignored my advice.

That evening the crew had all gone ashore; mainly to the various pubs around the town. Left on board was one sleepy engineer officer, and during this time the tide, driven on by the storm force southerly wind, rose more than four feet above its predicted height. Also the waves now rushing into the harbour lifted the ship well above the pier and the ladder the crew had used to get ashore soon disappeared into the water never to reappear. As the wind increased to storm force, the vessel was then moving violently up and down the pier, and the ropes

f

holding it fast began parting under the strain. Eventually, when all the ropes had parted, the drifting ship's bow narrowly missed landing on a launching slipway in that corner of the harbour and ran straight into the wall of the car park; and then with the force of wind and the ship moving it ended up bedded in the soft in-fill behind the retaining barrier. Meanwhile the stern, now high of the water, was still alongside the stone pier sustaining considerable damage.

I was, at this time, unaware of what was happening in Penzance. In fact, I was at a chapel meeting in St. Ives giving a talk. My wife arrived just as I was finishing, saying, "You're needed in Penzance as soon as possible!"

I arrived in the port, 10 miles away, some twenty minutes later. On the quay were the four harbour staff and two of the managers of the dry dock, but there were no crew to be seen. My first problem was to get aboard the ship which was now banging into the stone on her stern, but not moving as she was jammed in the corner. With the help of the dock head staff we managed to acquire a ladder from the dry dock company and I crawled across the space in the middle of ship to get on to the deck along with two of the dock staff.

Then, taking the parted ship's ropes, we tied bowline loops in them and passed them from the stern down on to the pier. At this point I discovered the engineer asleep in his cabin, and with some trouble got him to start a generator and give us power to work the ship's windlass at the bow and capstan at the stern. With these we successfully pulled the ship out of the hole in the car park and regained the proper berth on the pier.

Now we paused for a short rest, and that was a mistake. While we boiled a kettle the ship broke loose again and punched another hole in the car park before we could do anything about it.

I decided another approach might be needed and, before we tried again, I made an entry to the forward stores on the ship. There, to my amazement, I found two brand new ropes, and while we were still getting the ropes up to the deck the engineer arrived to find the ship still in the wrong position. As we struggled on deck and were getting the ropes fast, the engineer suddenly manoeuvred the engine astern and the ship came back from the car park and hit the quay with a loud thump. I ran for the engine room and yelled at the engineer to stop the engine, while the harbour staff held one of the new ropes at the bow.

Eventually we made the ship fast but all the time the wind was increasing. Following this we backed up the new ropes with the damaged ones once more as a precaution. A little while after this the entire crew appeared, having been at a drinking session in a local pub.

To my amazement they came aboard and, despite my efforts, all went to their cabins and locked the doors – including the captain.

By 2am the ship's movement parted one of the new ropes and I was forced to take desperate measures to stop the ship breaking adrift again. Lying on the pier were four very heavy wire rope moorings used by the *Scillonian*, and I made these fast to the ship. Three of these held but one did part before the vessel grounded in the berth at low tide at 3.30am. I stayed with the ship until 4am in the morning.

Four hours later I returned after taking some rest. The vessel was now coming afloat on the rising tide. By then the very worst of the storm had passed through, but the heavy movement of the tide and the condition of the vessel meant we could not move to another berth. At this time the captain remained behind his locked cabin door ignoring all attempts to wake him up.

It was not long before I was confronted by the manager of the Isles of Scilly Steamship Company, demanding I move the ship as the ferry *Scillonian II* required the berth. My advice to him was he should try to wake the master as I was only the pilot. After a few very angry words about my responsibility for this situation he took his leave and retired to complain to the Town Clerk of the Penzance Council, the harbour owners.

The said clerk arrived, and then left without satisfaction.

Then just after 10am the RMV *Scillonian* began blowing its whistle and calling me on the radio. Paul Rowe, the captain, was not pleased when I advised him (a master mariner like myself) of the state of the *Yewhill*. Therefore, due to the circumstances of

Force Majeure (a basic term for Act of God), the ship could not be moved. I also informed him that any loss caused by the incident would be met by the ship's insurance company, including the use and damage to his heavy duty moorings. As pilot I was able to say that there was just room for him to berth on the same pier as ourselves, or he could proceed to Hayle or Falmouth as he pleased.

After a lot of argument the *Scillonian* did berth astern of the *Yewhill* in safety. My total bill to the shipowner was £115 and the dock staff and Trinity House all had a cut out of that amount.

14

Manager of St. Ives
Lifeboat Station

In 1972 I was approached by the shipping agent in Penzance, a
Mr Dell Johnson, to see if I would become the secretary of the
St. Ives Lifeboat Station.. Then an interview was arranged with
Captain Porchmouth, the local Lifeboat Inspector. Despite my
reluctance, and with some pressure from Del (who pointed out
that as the ship's agent he paid me for many of my duties), I
agreed to take on the job which was entirely voluntary.

So, for the next ten years, the job of Trinity House pilot and
lifeboat secretary were to run parallel in my life, with the duties
and work merging on some occasions.

My first experience of the lifeboat was to come only a week
later, in fact, before I had even written a formal letter to the RNLI
accepting the position.

My predecessor as secretary was Captain Tommy Stevens and
he had sailed with my father in the Hain Line. Now over 73 years
of age he was long overdue for retirement but up till then no one
could be found to replace him.

Captain Porchmouth had been pressing me to take over all the
records and control of the St. Ives station. So as a south-east
storm had hit West Cornwall and the port of Penzance was closed
with my pilot boat safe behind the dock gates and out of
commission, I therefore visited Captain Stevens at his home in

Tregenna Terrace which had a wonderful view of the bay and St. Ives harbour. I could see that even in St. Ives Bay it was very rough and outside the headland of the harbour large waves were breaking with much force. We sat down to sort out the handover of control.

Tommy took his duties very seriously. In his hand, as I entered his home, he held his telephone which was on a very long lead and went with him wherever he was in the house. (Long before mobile phones, of course.) Now it was placed on the table ready to be answered as soon as it rang. He then produced a mass of paperwork connected with the lifeboat, including the wages and deductions of the full-time mechanic Douglas Hosking. He proudly told me that he did all the paperwork concerning the duties of the crew. I did not have the heart to tell him that I wasn't going to do all that work as well as earn a living. However, he did hand over all the operational telephone numbers and enlighten me as to his relationship with the local coastguards and crew of the lifeboat.

As we were chatting about his experiences sailing with my father the telephone rang. It was the coxswain of the lifeboat, Tommy Cocking, reporting that a local fishing boat, the *Trevose*, with John Veal and his son Brian had left the harbour earlier. They were fishing under the cliffs some 2/3 miles west of St Ives where there was shelter from the land. However, the conditions off St. Ives head would be dangerous for the *Trevose* on her return. Also the men would need assistance to place their catch of crabs in the keep nets off the harbour.

Captain Stevens at once agreed to launch the Lifeboat *Frank Penfold Marshall* to assist and stand by the vessel. He then informed Tommy that the new secretary elect would be coming with them.

So it was that five minutes later I was present at the lifeboat house dressing into sea boots and oilskins. The crew, of course, all knew me but now they were looking with interest and wondering whether I would be seasick on the forthcoming rescue.

It turned out to be lively but not too difficult. We found the *Trevose* two miles west of St. Ives just finishing fishing work. John was very grateful for the lifeboat assistance and the concern for his safety. It was soon all over and I then discovered it would take over three hours to recover the lifeboat due to tidal conditions. St. Ives harbour was without an RNLI mooring; the crew had to wait with the boat afloat until the tide had receded. Then the boat could be beached on soft sand and placed on the carriage to be returned to the lifeboat house.

I must say I was not impressed at that and promised the crew I would do something about it. That statement was received with scepticism. Tommy remarked: "We've been waiting for twenty years and can't see that happening in a hurry."

Three months later we had the mooring and it is still in use today.

By the way, and to the disappointment of the crew, I did not show any signs of discomfort from seasickness. I was soon to discover the ways of working and set about improving the performance of the station and its two lifeboats: the deep sea all weather boat *Frank Penfold Marshall* (a 37 foot Oakley class boat) and the inshore D-class lifeboat later to be called *Lion Cub One*.

15

A Wonderful Rescue

One way to describe the working of the lifeboat *Frank Penfold Marshall* is to relate a rescue of the ketch *Rosalind* on the 4th of August 1973.

That morning the rising sun had a glassy look as it rose over West Cornwall. Soon after dawn a gentle south west wind rippled the seas off St. Ives Head. Holidaymakers were on their way to the beaches, armed with their buckets and spades and the occasional rubber dinghy. St. Ives at the beginning of August had then, and still does have, a massive influx of visitors, so the two lifeboats tend to be very busy at that time of year.

As I ate my breakfast I listened to the latest weather forecast. The south-west wind was due to increase to a near gale during the day, and veer westerly increasing to a full gale by the evening. As I was a self-employed Trinity House pilot and there were no movements scheduled in Mount's Bay, I decided to stay at home in St. Ives. I could therefore attend to my duties as the local lifeboat secretary.

After breakfast I had a pleasant stroll down to the lifeboat house situated on the harbour front. I had now been carrying out this voluntary duty for some eight months and was, to be truthful, still getting used to the ways of lifeboatmen and the RNLI. On arrival I found both coxswain Tommy Cocking senior and mechanic Douglas Hosking in the lifeboat house checking the equipment and working parts of the lifeboat. Tommy informed me that the inshore duty helmsman William Benny was also doing the same at the inshore lifeboat house situated in the harbour car park some 200 yards away.

"All activity today then, Tommy," I said.

"Oh yes," said Tommy. "We will have a launch of one of the boats today, you see."

I could only comment that I hoped the people on the harbour and the beaches would notice the increasing wind and conditions. Flying from the piers of the harbour, red flags indicated that pleasure boats were not permitted to proceed that day.

I was to spend most of the day at the lifeboat house, breaking only for lunch and going home again around 5pm for my evening meal. During that time our volunteers kept appearing in the lifeboat house to ask if all was well. They were all expressing the opinion that we would have a launch before the day was out.

Meanwhile the wind was gaining in strength, but in the harbour and on the west side of St. Ives Bay it was sheltered and fairly calm. It took an experienced eye looking eastwards towards the far shore to notice the increasing white crests of waves rolling onto the beaches. Even so I felt no apprehension and was somewhat pleased to remark to Douglas, as I left the lifeboat house for my meal, that the lifeboatmen had not been disturbed so far. Douglas just muttered, "We'll see!"

During that morning, in Crowe Sound to the north and east of St. Mary's in the Isles of Scilly, a ketch called the *Rosalind* was at anchor sheltered from the south-west wind. The owner/skipper, a Mr Worth, had his wife, another couple and three children on board. They were sailing this brand new boat on her maiden voyage and had motored over to the islands from Falmouth the day before. The children were playing and fishing with lines, and the adults were enjoying the scenery and cooking a substantial breakfast. Just before midday they hauled up the anchor and set out for a passage to St. Ives Bay under motor alone. Although they did not know it they were already at risk and about to learn a harsh lesson in seamanship. Since taking over the boat they had not even put up the sails, but instead they had relied solely on the boat's engine. Now, as they proceeded, they did not realise that the anchor rope was not secure on the deck and one end was dangling over the side. Also they had made the fundamental mistake of not checking the weather forecast and were unaware that a gale was on the way.

All went well at first as the islands provided a certain amount of shelter and the wind was only just beginning to freshen from the south-westerly direction. So over the first couple of hours they made good progress past the Seven Stones Reef and on towards the high and forbidding cliffs of the north coast of Cornwall.

It was mid-afternoon when their troubles really began; the ketch was proceeding before a growing sea and swells. As the ketch moved and pitched, the anchor rope, bit by bit, slipped over the side until, with a resounding bang, the engine stopped with the rope wound tightly around the propeller. Now, as the ketch rolled helplessly in the swell, a worried skipper and his companions began to hoist the boat's sails. The jib quickly turned the *Rosalind* back on her course towards St. Ives and the main sail now provided the speed from the strong following wind to push the voyage on. However, the crew was unable to raise the mizzen sail and this meant that the ketch could only run before the wind, and this was to have very unfortunate consequences on arrival at St. Ives Bay.

Meanwhile at St. Ives, a Mr Atkins arrived with his family from Birmingham during the late afternoon. He could not wait to get his group down onto Porthminster Beach and try his 5 foot long rubber dinghy for a spot of fishing. By now the south-west wind was reaching near gale strength, but under the shelter of the land it did not seem too bad to this inexperienced holidaymaker. Unaware of just how unmanageable a rubber boat is in a gale of wind and a strong tidal current, he embarked, together with his ten year old son, on his fishing trip. At about 6.30pm, equipped with a couple of recently acquired lines, he was quite happy fishing off the beach. As it was now near high water, the rubber boat was afloat in a sheltered area and it did not drift too quickly over the first half hour as it was able to stay close to the shore.

However, with no fish around, Mr Atkins decided to put out further to sea.

St. Ives harbour limits were marked by a number of small buoys and Mr Atkins wanted to make fast his craft to one of them to resume fishing. It did not take long for the strong wind to sweep the little dinghy out into the bay. Despite the desperate efforts of Mr Atkins and his son they were swept away from the nearest buoy, and with the help of a strong tidal flow, straight past the harbour entrance towards the open sea.

In those days St. Ives had three permanent coastguard watch keepers and their duty ended that day at 8pm. So an experienced professional, 'Nobby' Clark, was on watch at the Island lookout as the little rubber boat was swept seawards. He phoned me at home just as I settled down after a good meal to watch some television.

"Eric, there's a very small rubber boat with a man and boy being swept past the head, and I would consider that the boat will not last more than ten minutes if it gets clear of the shelter in the bay. There's a considerable sea and swell running at the moment. Could you launch the inshore rescue lifeboat immediately, please?"

"On our way," was my reply.

Of course, I might have known Tommy was in the lifeboat house and sounded our klaxon alarm almost at once. The coxswain then ran to the inshore lifeboat house behind the Sloop Inn and got the lifeboat and carriage moving with the help of our head launcher Jimmy Benney. We did not have a tractor in those days and the boat and carriage had to be manhandled into the water.

Four minutes later helmsman William Benney, with David Smith and Tommy Cocking Jr, were afloat and on their way. It took the little D-class lifeboat just another four minutes to reach the rubber boat and grab it just as it was approaching the really rough seas. By this time I was at the lifeboat house myself and was in time to see the 16 foot lifeboat carrying two persons and the 5 foot boat back to the harbour. There followed a somewhat terse interview with Mr Atkins on the subject of rubber boats, offshore winds and local knowledge, followed by a cup of tea and a general feeling of relief around the lifeboat house.

A little later Tommy Cocking senior announced with some feeling, "There we are lads, all over for today. We were right about the launch, Eric."

I had to admit he was right, but suddenly I felt a feeling of doubt. Then almost as an afterthought, I said, "I don't think our day has finished yet Tommy, where are you for the rest of the evening?"

"Oh no," Tommy almost yelled. "I've booked a Chinese meal with the wife tonight and you will have to summon me with the maroons." (Rockets which announced the launching of our deep sea lifeboat in those days.)

"Same with me," said Douglas Hosking.

Jimmy Benney joined in: "I'm also out this evening."

These remarks only increased my unease. What if a quick launch was really needed? Still, as the boss, I kept my doubts to myself and proceeded homewards hoping I was wrong.

As I got home the *Rosalind* was approaching St. Ives Bay and making slow progress against a very strong ebb tide. The following wind had now veered to the west-south-west and increased to a full gale. Aboard the ketch steering was becoming very difficult as the rope around the propeller was also hindering the rudder. Just after nine o'clock Mr. Worth was to realise the very real difficulty he was in. He had turned across the wind on rounding St. Ives head but the ketch would not sail closer to the wind than a full ninety degrees due to the lack of a mizzen sail. So like it or not, and still against a strong tide, he sailed straight past St. Ives Harbour towards Hayle and the very dangerous estuary. Seeing the huge breakers ahead, he then altered his course down wind, and could only head straight for the beach at Gwithian on the east side of the bay where the breakers were just as bad.

Meanwhile at home, I was standing by the phone as it rang at twenty past nine. Mr. Stevens, a local fisherman, was on the other end.

"Eric, I am worried about the fishing boat *Shelder*, it has been

84

crabbing fifteen miles north-east of St. Ives Head and was due home at six o'clock and there is no sign of it."

"Right," I replied. "I'll check around with the coastguards and see if it has made for Newquay or Padstow for shelter. Not to worry, we'll launch the lifeboat and look for the boat if there is no information of its whereabouts."

At that time no watch was being kept by the coastguard at St. Ives and I phoned the lookout at Cape Cornwall, north of Land's End. My call went something like this:

"Good evening. I am concerned about the safety of a local St. Ives fishing vessel called the *Shelder*, it has been fishing some fifteen miles north-east of here and was due back at six this evening. It has not arrived. Could you enquire or ascertain if it has sought shelter at Newquay or Padstow?"

The watchman was very busy; he had the Lizard Lifeboat at sea for another yacht in trouble and a helicopter on its way to a medical call as well. "Don't hassle me now, I have enough on my plate," he replied.

As he spoke a voice seemed to say to me: "Launch the lifeboat now!" but nobody was in the room. My reaction was instantaneous:

"I am launching the lifeboat now. Please inform the Coastguard Station at St. Ives."

"Oh no!" said the bewildered watchkeeper.

It was as if I was in a dream: "Put the phone down, man," I barked with all the authority of a deep sea ship's captain – and he did!

My next call was to the second coxswain of the lifeboat Mike Peters, but there was no answer, the next available crewman was the second mechanic David Smith. He was one of those unflappable men who never seemed to hurry but was always there when you needed him.

"David, put the maroons off right away. The *Shelder* is missing. Move quickly, man."

"That's alright, Eric, I will be on my way shortly."

"Now!" I yelled.

"OK, OK. I'm on my way at once."

Then I phoned Melvin Veal our tractor driver, and a couple of the other members of the crew, before running down the road to the lifeboat station.

All those years ago it was quite a job to get the boat afloat. The lifeboat house was at right angles to the road around the harbour. The tractor driver had to remove the wheel chocks from the lifeboat carriage and then gently push the lifeboat on its carriage out onto the pier bow first. Then he would release the towing hook and proceed to turn the tractor around, reconnect and pull it at a fair speed along the front to the slipway in the middle of the harbour. Then the boat had to be uncoupled once more and the tractor placed in a position to push the boat into the sea. This took skill and nerve, and while it was happening the crew mustered, got dressed in their wet weather gear and life jackets, and boarded the boat prior to the tractor pushing the boat and carriage into the water. It is much quicker today, with a new lifeboat house, but it is still quite a manoeuvre, just the same.

On my arrival at the lifeboat house Melvin had started the tractor, various lifeboatmen had arrived including Tommy, Douglas and the others. The language was choice and the general opinion seemed to be that the Hon Sec had lost his marbles. The general chatter only increased when the local coastguard, Robbie Robbins, stopped his Land Rover outside to ask what the devil I was doing?

It was just after nine-thirty and Mr Worth could see and hear the surf booming ahead of his vessel, so he let off a red flare, burning his hand in the process. As the flare rose above the bay the lifeboat was moving at her fastest possible pace, the coastguard vehicle was racing ahead to the lookout, and all conversation ceased as if by magic. By nine-forty the lifeboat was on its way across the bay. The ketch with the sails now down was drifting towards the breaking surf. In actual fact the lifeboat caught up with *Rosalind* inshore of a set of treacherous rocks called the Bessacks and only feet from the breakers.

There was barely time to surge alongside the casualty, place a rope through the yacht's jib stay and pull it to deeper water. The ketch had missed the rocks by feet and all on the scene breathed a huge sigh of relief. Now the lifeboat was to tow the vessel back to St. Ives where harbour master Gordon Stevens and a massive crowd of visitors and locals alike waited to see the result of the lifeboat service.

There is a photograph in this book showing the three very frightened children saved from the sea. In those far-off days £100 was a lot of money and Mr Worth, after his injured hand had been dressed by the first aider John Bryant Thomas, presented £100 to the RNLI and £100 to share between the crew – some compensation for interrupted chinese meals and lost nights out while at sea. But for me the voice was critical, as a Christian I believe God spoke at that time. One thing is sure, if we had not been launching at the time of the red flare, those children might not have lived that night out.

As for the *Shelder*; the boat arrived in the bay shortly after with a loose rudder, and the lifeboat just stood by while it entered the harbour. All in all an eventful day!

The personnel in these rescues were as follows. *Lion Cub 1* D-class inshore rescue lifeboat crew: William Benney (coxswain), David Smith and Tommy Cocking Jr. *Frank Penfold Marshall* 39 foot Oakley lifeboat crew: Tommy Cocking Senior (coxswain), Douglas Hosking (mechanic), John Bryant Thomas (2nd coxswain), David Smith (2nd mechanic), Tommy Cocking Jr, John Tanner and William Benney. Head Launcher Jimmy Benney, Tractor Driver Melvin Veal and 12 other helpers.

16

Lifeboat Station Transformed

During the following years I spent much of my time working for better facilities both for the pilotage and lifeboat station. We were able to extend and improve the inshore lifeboat house, and provide a tractor with the help of the local Lions Club. Improved launching procedures made *Lion Cub 1* one of the fastest launching lifeboats in Britain, with consistent launches of less than 3 minutes and a record of 90 seconds, all due to the high morale of the fine body of men who served at that time.

In 1975 I sold the pilot boat *Grey Ling* and acquired a Trinity House workboat *Vestal* which had the power to tow vessels and carry cargo of up to two tons. We now carried lights and had a VHF radio, and were able to carry out much more work for the local council, and also work with ships that would have been impossible to cope with in my first years as a working pilot.

By 1977 the St. Ives Lifeboat Station had been transformed in its efficiency and contribution to inshore and offshore rescue. In those days the Sennen Cove lifeboat at Land's End could not launch for a period of two hours either side of low water. This meant that the only deep sea lifeboat available between Land's End and Newquay was the one at St. Ives. Therefore the station had plenty of work to do during this time.

With a much better call-out system, due to the hand-held radios between the launching authority and crews, the launching times getting to sea improved by a tremendous amount. On average the inshore lifeboat was at sea within three minutes of a call, and the deep sea lifeboat between 10 and 14 minutes. However, at this time, to launch the deep sea lifeboat still involved pulling the vessel halfway round the harbour road, and then down a slipway and into the sea.

With so many launches on service at this time the stories are too numerous to relate, but I will try to give you some examples which made my life really interesting and, dare I say, worthwhile.

MV *Fast Bird 2*

It was the 22nd of December 1977 and the weather had been consistently poor for over a week, with gales from a southerly direction throughout that time. In St. Ives Bay a small coaster called the *Grit*, of about 550 gross tons (and owned by a company called Everard Shipping based at Greenhithe, on the River Thames), had been sheltering from the elements. Some distance from the coaster and also sheltering was a Greek cargo ship the *Fast Bird 2*, registered in Piraeus. This ship had no cargo on board and was on passage from Dakar in Senegal to Fowey on the south coast of Cornwall. It was an old German built ship and was a substantial size, being 3521 gross tons. Indeed, we were surprised that the captain should have decided to come to the bay at all when Falmouth was on her route to Fowey. Outside the bay the large fish factory ship *Conqueror*, registered in Grimsby, was also sheltering but unable to anchor and so moving around along the sheltered coastline. During the morning the Hull fish factory vessel *Junella* joined the two other ships in the bay to avoid the worst sea conditions from the storm to come. Throughout the rest of the day the sea conditions grew worse, with a big swell building and coming from the west.

At 2.30pm the St. Ives lifeboat *Frank Penfold Marshall* launched for a training exercise. This proved a very rare situation, as normally Coxswain Tommy Cocking would not let his deputy take the boat except if he was ill or away, but on this occasion 2nd Coxswain Newell Perkin was to take charge. Also aboard, as well as the normal crew members, were a local policeman, a coastguard officer from the Plymouth area and a Canadian reporter.

The MV *Grit* was running short of provisions, including fresh water, so the lifeboatmen, showing Christmas goodwill, delivered some fresh water and seasonal food to the crew of the vessel which was now at the mercy of the weather.

After this the lifeboat carried out man overboard training, navigational procedures and various radio tests with the coastguards. So by 6.25pm the lifeboat was approaching the harbour to be recovered to the trailer.

Tommy Cocking was watching events from the pier and I was at home listening to my mobile VHF radio when I heard the voice of Mr Clark, the local coastguard, broadcasting on the emergency channel.

"*Fast Bird 2*, what are you doing?" and this was repeated three times.

The lifeboat, just short of grounding on the harbour sand, went astern on its engines, stopping progress and waiting. Tommy Cocking could be heard shouting at the top of his voice for the lifeboat to let him aboard. Aware of the urgency in Mr Clark's voice, I continued listening very intently indeed.

Meanwhile the coastguard looked on in disbelief as the ship steamed towards the very rough sea and swell outside the bay, then turned a half circle at full speed and made straight towards the beach on the south side of the entrance of the port of Hayle.

Suddenly a broad Greek voice announced on the radio that the ship had parted her anchor, was not able to steer, the engine was jammed at full speed ahead and the vessel was running ashore. Then after a slight pause, "Get me a tug!"

The lifeboat immediately turned away from the harbour and headed in the direction of the runaway ship. On the pier at St. Ives the coxswain was almost beside himself at not being on the lifeboat at such an important time. I had run, in the gathering darkness, to my motor scooter and five minutes later joined Nobby Clark in the coastguard lookout.

Across the bay the lights of the ship could be seen well inside those of the small coaster the *Grit*. It was to emerge later that no one on that ship had observed the grounding as they were all enjoying a good meal – the first for a couple of days.

Just after I arrived the lifeboat put up a white flare and illuminated the scene. We could see the ship aground very close to the local golf course with the engine still going full speed ahead. Repeated calls from the lifeboat had failed to get any reaction from the ship. As we looked on, the lifeboat radio operator reported a large crowd of crew members shouting from the main deck where a pilot ladder had been placed over the side. With some difficulty coxswain Newel Perkin manoeuvred the lifeboat to a position close to the ladder. Already the storm was increasing and conditions alongside were not good. Now, on Newel's orders, two members of the crew, Eric Ward and Tommy Cocking Jr, jumped on to the ladder, and as the now growing swell threatened to damage the lifeboat, Newel backed off to allow Eric to assess the situation.

On deck Eric and Tommy Jr (just 16 years old at the time) faced the tricky decision of what to do. Firstly Eric told young Tommy to go to the bridge and find out the captain's intentions and then report to the lifeboat coxswain. Meanwhile he pushed his way through the crowd of crew members on the ship and made his way to the engine room. On his way he checked the 2nd engineer's cabin, where he came across an engineer packing a suitcase. Eric was, at this time, a tall and strong policeman and he grabbed the engineer and dragged him to the engine room door. Below them the engine was running at full speed with no one in attendance. Eric indicated to the man, by drawing his hand across his own throat, the order to stop the engine. The man immediately climbed down the engine room ladder and stopped the engine.

Meanwhile young Tommy Cocking Jr had arrived on the ship's bridge, and finding no one there he called Newel on the lifeboat to tell him the news. Newel was rather short with his reply: "Carry on quickly Tommy, search the accommodation, find him and ask his intentions."

Directly below the bridge Captain George Spithogiannis lived in a large spacious cabin. Tommy found a curtain covering the open door and nervously pulled it aside. Inside the captain had a large suitcase on a table and he was packing it with passports and other documents.

"Excuse me, sir," said Tommy Jr, "I am from the lifeboat. . ."

His sentence was then cut off by the captain shouting, "Lifeboat? We are abandoning the ship!"

Tommy fled to the bridge where he called Newel once more with the news.

At this point the St. Ives coastguard broke into the conversation. "Request you obtain details of how many crew as soon as possible."

Five minutes later Tommy returned to the radio. "Newel, there are 15 Greeks, 7 Indians and 2 Pakistanis."

That just about stunned everyone listening as young Tommy returned to the ship's main deck.

Newel now had the task of putting the lifeboat alongside the ship's pilot ladder while the two lifeboatmen on board organised the crew in suitable positions on deck. By this time the crew, including the captain, had collected a large amount of suitcases (already packed) and piled them alongside the pilot ladder. As the lifeboat came alongside it damaged its deck rails because the swell pushed the boat violently against the ship, but now the crew of the lifeboat could get a bowline on to the freighter. Just as they were doing this the captain threw his suitcase down on to the lifeboat's deck, where it burst open spilling passports all over. At once the passengers and a couple of the crew hurried down to catch the passports before they were washed away, then almost immediately three more suitcases were thrown down on to the lifeboat.

Eric knew at this point that he had to take action or lives could be lost. Standing at his full height he placed himself in front of the shouting and panicking crew and physically stopped the group from their actions. As Eric took control, order returned to the deck and the men at his command formed a line.

The captain then jumped on to the ladder and climbed down to the waiting lifeboat. When he jumped aboard, however, he sprained his ankle; which I suppose was a little justice for the whole situation for which he was responsible.

As the crew was being brought back to the harbour the two lifeboatmen were left on board to check if there was anyone else on board. It was not long before we were informed that a dog had been found in the engineer's accommodation. That had to be left on board due to the quarantine regulations for a vessel coming from Dakar in West Africa.

Meanwhile on shore there were problems I had to confront. For the first time in twenty years we had to cope with a large group of survivors.

As the lifeboat house was not able to cope with so many survivors in those days, I requested the help, through the chairperson Marion Pearce, of the Ladies of the Guild and members of the Salvation Army whose building was next to our lifeboat house. They together made the mariners comfortable as we were trying to find somewhere for them to stay.

For this purpose I had to contact the shipping agent in Penzance, Del Johnson. On the 23rd of December there is a celebration called Tom Bawcock's Eve in Mousehole, a village close to Penzance, and Del was just leaving to join in the celebration prior to that event when I phoned him. To say he was not amused was an understatement. With nowhere else available for the sailors, he had to organise a bus which would collect the crew to stay at a posh hotel in Penzance.

In the meantime the lifeboat, now with Tommy Cocking Sr in command, had removed the two lifeboatmen and the crews' luggage and returned to the lifeboat station.

When the crew from MV *Fast Bird 2* were first brought to the Salvation Army Citadel, Captain George Spithogiannis joined the local coastguard and myself to give us an explanation for the whole sorry event. That proved impossible and all he would say, as he clutched his foot, was: "I don't care. All our crew are safe and I am proud of myself." So we let him join his crew and left them to the agent's care.

Finally, I had to contact the RNLI at Poole to request the repair of the minor damage to the rails on the lifeboat and that they fix an engine pump that was giving trouble. Then it was home from a job well done – or so I thought.

The storm was getting rapidly worse, with driving rain and increasing wind speed. The local coastguard was ordered to mount a watch over the wreck of *Fast Bird 2*, and they did this in their emergency Land Rover parked on the fairway of the local golf club. At this time the crew members of the MV *Grit* were still totally unaware of the drama that had taken place around them.

At this point I must admit to being wrong in my opinion of the situation. A reporter from Radio Cornwall had phoned me early in the evening and asked about the stranded freighter. I had advised that it was unlikely the vessel would be salvaged quickly as vessels on Hayle Bar normally sank into the sand and were then difficult to refloat. So, based on this information, the reporter made plans to see the wreck at first light. However, *Fast Bird 2* was not finished with us yet and the remarkable story was soon to take a new turn.

By midnight that day the weather conditions had deteriorated even further and the approaching high tide meant that the depth of water at the wreck site was higher than predicted. I was listening to my radio receiver in case of any other mariners being in trouble. Just after midnight I heard the captain of the MV *Grit* calling the St. Ives Coastguard Station. The conversation went as follows:

"St. Ives coastguard, there's a vessel moving inside my position."

At once the coastguard replied, "There is no vessel inside your position, *Grit*."

The captain then went on to say, "Yes there is."

"The only vessel inside of you is the *Fast Bird 2* and that vessel is aground on the beach near Hayle."

There followed a snort from the captain, then, "Well it is not aground now, it is drifting towards this ship."

After a short silence there followed a startled coastguard reply, "Can you tow her sir?"

"No, I've been here a week looking after myself and I cannot attempt to tow a vessel of that size."

At that moment the skipper of the fishing factory ship *Junella* came on the air saying he would get his vessel underway and tow *Fast Bird 2*.

Now this was of interest to me, and I immediately phoned the St. Ives coastguard with this question: "Please ask the *Junella* Skipper how his vessel will tow the *Fast Bird 2* and how will he make the line fast on the ship?"

It turned out that the skipper intended to ask one of his crew to jump as he approached the drifting ship. This was a very dangerous procedure, so I used my right to launch the lifeboat and ordered coxswain Tommy to assist *Junella* rather than risk a man's life given the storm conditions in the bay.

While this was happening the coastguard at St. Ives was frantically calling the coastguard parked in his Land Rover on the golf course without result.

Ten minutes later the *Fast Bird 2* drifted slowly past the *Grit* with the wind effect overcoming the tidal flow towards the Hayle estuary.

At that point the coastguard in his Land Rover called the St. Ives coastguard to report that the freighter had gone and asking for instructions. He was told to proceed to Godrevy Point, near the lighthouse at the north-east point of the bay.

As the lifeboat approached the now moving *Junella*, Tommy asked the skipper of the *Junella* what help he needed.

"For a start, coxswain, how deep is the water towards Godrevy Point?" (This is where *Fast Bird 2* was now heading.)

Tommy then asked the skipper, "How deep is your vessel in the water, sir?"

"19 feet 6 inches," was the reply.

Tommy's advice was dramatic to say the least: "Go astern or you will be aground sir."

That was the end of the fishing vessel's attempt at salvage. I was about to recall the lifeboat when the coastguard Land Rover arrived at the Godrevy site and the officer reported that the freighter *Fast Bird 2* would soon be on the rocks.

However, the ship had now emerged into an area where the wind was more effective and the current was easing on the high water. Miraculously, just before the vessel would have been wrecked, it altered direction enough to avoid the rocks at Godrevy Point and Godrevy Island itself. Helped on by a change of wind direction to the south-west it sailed serenely through a channel between the lighthouse and the fearsome Stones reef.

I was speaking to the coastguard at the St. Ives lookout at the time and I thought he made a really appropriate remark on the whole incident:

"Cor! That dog is sure steering a brilliant course."

Of course, the dog found by the lifeboatmen was the only living soul on the boat!

When I then requested that the lifeboat return to station the order was not acted upon, however, because at that moment HMS *Shevington* arrived on the scene. The Royal Navy Commander countermanded my instructions as he assumed the post of on scene commander. He requested the lifeboat to place two lifeboatmen on the freighter along with two of his crew. In very poor conditions Tommy achieved this task and a ship's rope was attached to the Royal Navy minesweeper. Almost at once the rope parted, but then the commander on *Shevington* succeeded in getting a wire towing hawser in position and began to tow *Fast Bird 2* out into the Bristol Channel.

I then requested the lifeboat be released, and after the two lifeboatmen and navy crew reboarded their respective vessels, the St. Ives lifeboat returned to its station.

My parting advice to the minesweeper personnel was that the *Fast Bird 2* had engines in working order to help the tow. Unfortunately the Royal Navy found it impossible to use them because there were only German language instructions on their operation available. Two hours later the towing wire of the HMS *Shevington* parted and the salvage attempt ceased.

Next morning a frigate attempted to tow the ship with little success. Then on Christmas morning an admiralty tug, which had come from Plymouth, found *Fast Bird 2* drifting in flat calm sea conditions five miles from the entrance to Milford Haven. The vessel was therefore taken to that port.

I wonder still if this epic voyage of the *Fast Bird 2* was the longest navigation feat ever achieved by a dog? The crew of the *Fast Bird 2* stayed in Penzance until the 10th of January and then, with a new captain, they again took control of their runaway vessel. It was a coincidence that 8 months later the *Fast Bird 2* was in collision with another vessel off North Africa and sank – while the owners claimed on their insurance, I presume!

The *Lady Camilla* Tragedy

During the time that *Fast Bird 2* was drifting around in the Bristol Channel, a far more serious situation was developing some 30 miles north of St. Ives Bay. Just after midnight a small Danish coaster, *Lady Camilla*, 499 gross tons, reported that the tarpaulins covering its forward cargo compartment had been ripped. At that time the ship was experiencing a south-westerly severe gale force 10 with hurricane gusts reaching 100 knots. The cargo space was now filling with water, and the ship required immediate assistance.

The coastguards had ordered the launch of a helicopter from the Culdrose Air Station, near Helston, and two lifeboats – one from Clovelly (the largest and best the RNLI had at that time) and the other from Padstow – both of which were larger than the St. Ives boat *Frank Penfold Marshall*.

I was informed at 36 minutes past midnight that the two boats had launched under the emergency regulations. At once I questioned the wisdom of the decision to send two lifeboats from the east when our local lifeboat would be running with the weather and was the closest to the incident. After a delay of 5 minutes a senior coastguard admitted they were afraid to send an open lifeboat. I informed the officer that such a decision lay with the secretary and lifeboat coxswain at St. Ives. After some hesitation the St. Ives lifeboat also launched on the instruction of both myself and the coxswain.

I estimated the drift of the now sinking vessel and Tommy set off on a northerly course. By 2.20am he had reached a position 14 miles north of St. Ives, by far the closest boat to the casualty. The helicopter had been forced to land at Newquay airport, but due to adverse weather conditions was then unable to get airborne again.

Then a member of the public reported a red flare low on the horizon at Perranporth near Newquay, and the coastguard,

97

without contacting me, ordered the St. Ives coxswain to proceed to that position.

Tommy now had a very dangerous task, as he had to turn the lifeboat across a raging sea and swell. In the pitch darkness he could not see the very large swells until they broke right over the boat in all their fury. The crew members were sheltering in the cockpit of the boat with the watertight door between them and the engine room. As the boat turned, a massive swell broke right over the boat swamping the cockpit, the boat rolled over to 90 degrees and inside the space most of the men were under water. Tommy did keep his head above water and his son remained in an air pocket from his waist up along with the boat's VHF radio. Two lifeboatmen, including Newell Perkin the 2nd coxswain, were washed out of the boat and then back into safety as it righted itself.

The lifeboat was damaged; the VHF radio was working but all the lights, including those for navigation, had been extinguished. The compass still operated, but as the light did not function it proved necessary to shine a watertight torch beam for the coxswain to see the compass and steer the boat. These brave men then completed a search of the inshore area with no results whatsoever.

Out in the storm the *Lady Camilla* sank and four of the crew, including the captain's wife, managed to get into a life-raft. Sadly this was later found empty further up the north Cornwall coast. All aboard were lost, while the other two lifeboats found nothing.

I believe to this day that the report of a red flare was a sighting of the red flash of Trevose Lighthouse. I also believe that those poor people in the life-raft could have been saved by our lifeboat had the decision not been given to turn about, but nevertheless the bravery of the lifeboat crew themselves was outstanding.

When the report of the launch reached the RNLI they awarded Tommy Cocking a Silver medal and each of the crew congratulations on velum. The presentation was made in London and it was a great day for us as the Duke of Kent presented the medal to Tommy in the Royal Festival Hall.

17

'I Require a Pilot'

There have been a number of times in my life when my duties as a Trinity House pilot became combined with the lifeboat to assist vessels in danger. One such incident occurred on the 7th of December 1981, when the auxiliary coastguards set a bad weather watch at 7pm, with a south-west gale and very rough sea conditions outside St. Ives Bay. Using their radar at the station (they had raised the money locally for both a direction finder and the radar set) they observed, proceeding across the bay, an unknown vessel. As they watched, the ship altered course and headed for the Stones reef close to Godrevy Lighthouse. Frantic calls were then made to the vessel to change direction, and possibly as a result of these instructions, the vessel altered her course and made straight for the most dangerous part of the reef. The watching coastguard then sent up a flash and sound maroon, and at that point the captain must have noticed the rocks. Just in time the vessel altered direction and ran right along the edge of this reef without touching anything.

Following this the master tried to make contact with Land's End Radio on VHF, and from this call the coastguard was able to identify the ship as *Miss Tita*, registered in Limassol, Cyprus at 943 gross tons. The captain, at that time, was only willing to talk to the radio operator at Land's End Radio Station and was asking for a pilot. However, he would not change his radio frequency from the emergency channel. This meant the radio station was unable to contact him on a channel connected to the telephone.

It was at that point that the operator at Land's End, Richard King, contacted me and informed me of the situation. As I held a Trinity House Pilotage certificate for St. Ives Bay and Richard still could not persuade the captain to change his calling channel, I undertook to contact the vessel directly. At this point I handed my launching responsibility over to my deputy Captain Proudfoot and asked his permission to use the lifeboat radio (for which I held a radio licence) to make radio contact with the ship. This was granted by Dennis and I then made my way to the lifeboat house. By this time *Miss Tita* had turned around and was very slowly heading back towards the reef.

Boarding the lifeboat in the station I turned on the VHF radio and called *Miss Tita*, identifying myself as the St. Ives pilot. I received an answer right away and at my request the master changed his channel to the pilotage channel 9. I then informed the captain to steer to the north-west at slow speed and meanwhile I would request the help of the lifeboat to bring me out to the vessel's position.

Dennis agreed a launch to help me as I had no pilot boat at St. Ives. So it was that the crew all mustered and began moaning at me. It seems they were annoyed that they only received a small sum for launching and they considered that I would earn a fortune for my services as pilot. The point that I never got paid anything as secretary except my lifeboat telephone calls was lost on them. I just kept silent and let them ramble on.

As the lifeboat approached the ship it was obvious that, with the heavy swell and sea conditions, I was not going to be able to board.

Tommy grinned as he asked me, "What to do now then, Eric, do you want me to try and get you aboard?"

"No," I replied, "get the lifeboat into position ahead of the struggling vessel and I will talk to him on the radio."

The captain soon agreed to follow us and I was able to board the freighter as it reached the sheltered waters of the bay.

I got on board at 10.35pm and once on the deck I made for the bridge. I found a very tall African at the ship's wheel looking somewhat frightened, a young 22 year old gentleman standing by the wheelhouse windows and an older gentleman of between 40/50 years of age standing by a chart table. I wrongly assumed that the older man was the captain, but he protested strongly that he was the shoreside engineer. I next turned to the younger man and he confirmed he was indeed in command. I then directed the ship to a safe anchorage in the bay before asking the captain how he had managed to get into such a mess. He explained that his only chart showed the entire near continent from Germany to France as well as Britain and Ireland. St. Ives Bay on the chart was so small you needed a very big magnifying glass to make out anything. The Stones reef and other dangers were not named or prominent. It was no wonder he did not understand the directions given by the coastguards at St. Ives.

In the meantime the older man at the rear of the bridge was demanding to be put ashore. As I was not in control of the lifeboat at this point I directed him to go and shout to the coxswain who was waiting in the lifeboat close by. I advised the captain to contact the ship's agent Del Johnson at Penzance, to arrange a boat to bring out charts and stores next day. While I was talking to the captain, a deal had been struck by the so-called engineer (I suspected he was the owner really) and the lifeboat crew. This meant that, by the time I got aboard to go home to St. Ives, most of the crew were sporting cartons of cigarettes or bottles of booze. No more complaints now at the pilot using the lifeboat!

Miss Tita was bound from Oldenburg in Germany to Bideford and continued the voyage with correct charts two days later.

18

Royal Visitors

In the years from 1970 to 1999 I was to meet a number of the Royal Family. My first occasion, in the early nineteen seventies, was as Secretary of the St. Ives Lifeboat Station, when I stood with my wife in a special enclosure at Falmouth. Although only a couple of feet away from the Queen, I was for once (very rarely for me) lost for words as she shook hands with those standing there.

I must admit I was very proud to show off the local lifeboat station to the Duke of Kent (which included a trip in the lifeboat round the bay). He seemed to enjoy the launch procedure, which involved the lifeboat, on its carriage, being towed along the harbour road to the slipway. During this time crowds of people were cheering and clapping as we passed them on the road before we launched.

Then, of course, I was present in London on two occasions at the presentation of RNLI medals to Tommy Cocking and Eric Ward by the Duke of Kent. During these awards my wife and I met the duke again and talked for some time.

Another special occasion was the opening of the first section of the Mary Williams Pier in the port of Newlyn, when I had the honour, along with my partner pilot Captain Mike Sutherland, of being presented to the Queen and being able to talk to her about the shipping we handled at the port. In fact, at that time, I had assisted the Dutch salvage tug *Willem Barendsz* to come alongside the south pier, and the crew had dressed overall with flags and ensigns to greet the Queen.

Mike Sutherland had joined me in 1978 as the then Newlyn Pilot Les Davies had retired. Mike remained to take an active role during the very busy time after the Penzance and Newlyn pilotage had been merged.

However, it was after Mike left to be a harbour master in Fowey that I had my next meeting with royalty. In fact, I took over on my own in 1983, just before Easter, and now covered all the tasks originally carried out by three pilots.

At the end of October I had been very busy with six ships in three days, as well as landing a sick fisherman with a bad back from a Dutch deep sea trawler called the *Jan Maria*. After an examination at the local hospital he was sent home to Holland suffering from gout. The salvage tug *Fairplay X* had also arrived very early in the morning following a salvage task in Portugal, so I had been busy running mail and stores and custom officers out in the bay during the morning. At midday a thick fog had settled over the area, and I was sitting in my pilotage office taking it easy and staring out of the window on wharf road. Suddenly I noticed, in the gloom, the clerk who worked in the harbour office running towards me.

He arrived in the office in a breathless condition and announced that the harbour master wanted to see me right away.

Martin Tregoning was all smiles when he said, "HMS *Shetland* needs to berth on the Lighthouse Pier at 7.30pm tonight Eric, and we need your services."

"Out of the question," I announced with reason. "There will not be enough depth of water to bring the ship in, Martin."

"We have an important passenger to land, Eric, and this is urgent," responded the harbour master.

As it happened, the next day there was to be a memorial service for the late Earl Mountbatten in London and I knew who the important person was.

"Come on, Martin. It's the Prince of Wales, isn't it?"

Very reluctantly the harbour master agreed. The Prince had

been present in the Isles of Scilly and the *Scillonian III* was already berthed in Penzance.

I placed both of my pilot boats outside the dock basin, and then began a supreme effort by my boatmen Selwyn Jolly and Leo Downing, together with my son Ian, to scrub and clean the boats fit for a royal passenger. By 5.30pm we were ready, having had a meal together in a small transport café near the station, so just to see if the boat's radar could indicate a vessel had arrived in the bay, given the thick fog still prevailing at six o'clock, I moved the pilot boat *Medway* clear of the pier to observe the bay outside the port. As we looked at the screen there was an echo of the right size in the right place.

I then called HMS *Shetland* to see if it was possible to land the passengers early. I was promptly informed by the officer of the watch to do as ordered and come alongside at 7.30pm precisely.

Therefore, at exactly the prescribed time, the Penzance pilot boat *Vestal* was alongside to load the luggage of which there was a substantial amount. Before the loading commenced, a detective climbed down to supervise the stowage of the items which filled the cargo capacity of the boat. Lastly, a briefcase was lowered with the royal coat of arms emblazoned on the flap. The detective told Leo, "This is the most important item I safeguard."

Then Selwyn placed the pilot boat *Medway* alongside the pilot ladder and seven passengers, including the Steward of the Duchy of Cornwall, descended before Prince Charles himself climbed aboard. Our conversation was a very relaxed one, and I soon realised that the Prince had a keen sense of humour.

To make conversation I had related a story of a Dutch fisherman who we had landed the previous Christmas. We found him grasping a metal ventilator, kissing it and saying, "I love you, darling." Up until that moment no one had been able to move him but his strange actions meant he must leave his ship. He spoke English well, however, and I was able to suggest that the ship's agent Del Johnson, sitting below in the pilot boat and dressed in a thick fur-lined coat, was his girlfriend. He agreed at once and allowed us to get him down into the *Medway* without trouble. Of course, we were well aware he wanted to get home for Christmas. The mental hospital confirmed his sanity next day and Del arranged his transport home.

Prince Charles then asked me who was paying for my services on this occasion, and I replied, "The Duchy of Cornwall, sir." The Prince then called the Steward of the Duchy and informed him of my intention. The Steward promptly denied that the Duchy was paying anything. Prince Charles asked what I thought about that.

"Well sir, in that case I will make even more money telling the Fleet Street papers what you have said." It caused quite some laughter and I was paid at the end of the month.

On arrival at Penzance the dock staff helped my men carry the luggage to the Prince's car, but the detective forgot the Prince's briefcase. It was quite embarrassing as Leo shouted in front of the people watching that the detective had forgotten the Prince's sandwiches!

19

An Unexpected Summer Rescue

Wednesday the 26th of August 1981 proved to be a quiet sunny day. On the north coast in St. Ives Bay only the slightest breath of wind rippled the blue water of the sea. On the beaches and around the harbour at the resort, holidaymakers were enjoying the warm sun and bathing in the still waters. At the inshore lifeboat house, situated in the harbour car park, the duty coxswain Philip Allen had checked over the equipment of *Lion Cub 1*, and he was now enjoying a pasty before settling down to some sunbathing on the harbourside. Strapped to his belt was a portable receiver, allowing him to listen for any messages from the lifeboat secretary should he be needed. However, Philip considered that on such a fine day he would be having a quiet afternoon. His only concern was the large number of holidaymakers now settling down on the harbour slipway to enjoy the sun and have a picnic. He would have to clear a path between them should the inshore lifeboat be needed, so he informed as many people as possible on the slip that they must move should they hear the klaxon sound from the lifeboat house close by. As it happened it was a wise precaution as the D-class lifeboat was to launch twice that afternoon.

At the same time, some three miles to the west of St. Ives and situated high above the coastal footpath, John King, a holidaymaker from Twickenham in London, was admiring the view below, and enjoying a picnic lunch. To his left were the forbidding rocks called the Western Carracks and known to many visitors as Seal Island. These showed the only movement of water as the flowing tidal current swept past in an easterly direction. On the rocks the seals were enjoying the sun and the quiet, while the boats with their sightseers were not present. In front of John the path hugged the cliff edge for a short distance, and beyond he could see the sea changing colour from a light green to the dark blue of the deeper water further off the coast. Above the path the brown colour of the bracken was in complete contrast with the sea. To his right a small stream ran down a narrow wooded valley to plunge over the cliff in a waterfall to the sea below. The coastal footpath continued beyond the stream and climbed to an imposing point of land which cut off any further view of St. Ives.

It was about half past one in the afternoon when John noticed an imposing figure striding out on the footpath from St. Ives. As the man approached the path below, John could see that he was wearing just a pair of shorts with leather sandals on his feet and in his right hand he appeared to be carrying a document case. Right in front of John one of the many small coves carved a V shape in the cliff which led up to the coastal path itself.

For just a moment, as the passing walker was approaching, John's gaze was distracted by the beautiful sight of gannets diving on a passing shoal of fish. When he looked back at the coastal path there was no sign of the walker. Now all was quiet with nobody moving on the footpath within his view.

Alarmed, John made a dash for the coastal path, pushing aside the bracken and brambles to take a direct route to where he had last seen the walker. The cliffs at this point had a considerable overhang and it was impossible to see if the man was below. No answer was forthcoming to his shouts and no other human was visible to help, so it was a case of getting help as quickly as possible.

John had no means of communication, with no mobile phones in those days, and he faced a cruel uphill race of nearly a mile through the wooded valley to the nearest house at Trevail Bottoms. Some fifteen minutes later he was on the phone explaining to the Maritime Coastguard Station Officer at Falmouth just what he had seen.

Action quickly followed John's phone call. An urgent message went to the Royal Naval Air Station Culdrose at Helston, asking for the assistance of a search and rescue helicopter, while the St. Ives coastguard asked for the assistance of the St. Ives inshore lifeboat.

As the helicopter got under way from Culdrose, it was all action in the harbour at St. Ives. Philip Allen was already running the short distance from the slipway to the lifeboat house behind the Sloop Inn as his radio receiver relayed the information from myself that a man was over the cliffs some 3 miles west of St. Ives. The tractor driver John Stevens, who worked at the Inn alongside the inshore lifeboat house, had responded to Philip's call at once. Indeed he was towing the lifeboat *Lion Cub 1* with the tractor (named Tigger) towards the slipway as the Klaxon sounded at the main lifeboat house. My son Ian Kemp, the second launcher, was already moving people from the slipway as the boat appeared around the corner. Seemingly from nowhere, two crewmen, Ian Tanner and Ian Lowe, had arrived to grab their life jackets and man the lifeboat. With the flowing tide filling the harbour the inshore craft was soon afloat and on the way. Indeed it was a really remarkable launch carried out in just over one minute. As far as I know, the fastest ever for the station from a standing start!

The helicopter and lifeboat arrived almost together and commenced searching the cliffs for the missing man. In fact, both passed the gully in the cliff without seeing anything.

After a short time the helicopter returned to the map reference given by John King. One of the crewmen from the helicopter was lowered to the exact spot. There, at the rear of the inlet, hidden by the considerable overhang of the cliff, he found the man lying in a pool of blood and suffering from severe head injuries. He at once indicated to the aircraft that a stretcher should be lowered to lift the casualty out and he also asked for the help of the lifeboat crew.

As soon as the stretcher had been lowered and the helicopter moved away, the inshore lifeboat was able, in the flat calm conditions, to cruise into the cove. Then leaving their boat resting on the rocky shore without any danger of damage or it floating away, the crew waded chest deep around some outlying rocks and helped the airman to bring the stretcher to the injured man. Then followed the tricky job of lifting the casualty onto the stretcher and moving him down to the shoreline clear of the overhanging cliff. The helicopter swooped back in to remove the casualty and crewman, and then fly as fast as possible to Treliske Hospital at Truro some 25 miles away.

So in just under an hour from the first alarm call the casualty was in hospital, the helicopter had returned to base at Helston and the inshore lifeboat was back in its house and being washed down by its enthusiastic crew. After congratulating the crew and gathering the facts, I returned home to write out a report of the whole rescue and enjoy the rest of the afternoon.

I did not have the gentleman's name etc., but I expected the coastguard would be calling me with the details later in the day.

I was not surprised, therefore, at half past four to receive a call from Falmouth coastguard, but the information they gave me was worrying, to say the least. The rescued man had been in a critical condition and had been transferred by helicopter to Freedom Fields Hospital in Plymouth and subsequently to a Bristol hospital because of the severity of his injuries. Now Bristol had a problem, because they were unable to give the right treatment unless they could find out who the man was and locate his medical records. Our information had stated that the man had been carrying a document case and the coastguard service were requesting that our inshore lifeboat return to the scene to see if they could locate it.

So once more, still in flat calm conditions, Philip and his merry men launched on service and proceeded to the incident site again. There the crew scrambled ashore and made an intensive search of the cliff gully and waterside where the injured man had been found, with no result. After an hour of searching and in desperation Philip searched in the calm waters off the cove. Over half a mile out to sea the crew found the document case floating with just a tiny corner visible above the water.

Then followed a rapid return to St. Ives harbour, where the case was transferred to the local police station. There I met up with the crew and watched the duty police sergeant open the bulging case. It had remained waterproof, and out tumbled a camera, a full set of drawing pencils, paint brushes, some oil paints and some beautiful drawings of nude young ladies. Then, at the very bottom of the bag, was a small bottle of pills, and on the label was the name D. Field, Charing Cross Hospital. At once the police sergeant phoned the hospital and was connected with their dispensing department.

"My dear man," the voice from the other end of the telephone echoed, "we have over two thousand people registered here as out patients. Why do you wish to know?"

However, when acquainted with the urgent need to know at Bristol, the hospital staff pulled out all the stops. Some twenty minutes later we were informed that a search had located the complete records of Mr Field and these had been faxed to Bristol, and an operation on the gentleman was about to begin. Again I had to congratulate the lifeboat crew on a job really well done and in the true spirit of the RNLI.

It was a year later that a completely recovered Mr Field visited the lifeboat house. He personally thanked the lifeboat crew and all the others that had participated in his rescue a year before.

Such meetings really did give a boost to those of us who helped in the work of the lifeboat station. However, as we pointed out at the time, it was due to the sharp eyes and determination of Mr John King, and his punishing run back up the wooded valley, that the rescue was made possible. Yes, and he had missed the main action at the cove by the time he returned, due to the speed in which the rescue services had acted. For us the lesson was clear: whatever the weather you always had to be ready for a rescue call.

20

The Unfortunate Outcome
of a Brilliant Rescue

It was the Thursday before Good Friday in 1982, one of those sunny clear days ruined by a cold 30 knot northerly wind in St. Ives Bay. After my midday meal I walked down to the lifeboat house on the harbour front. Out in the bay the blue and green of the sea was disturbed by the white plumes of breaking waves running towards the Hayle estuary. Red flags were flying from the harbour piers preventing pleasure boats working that day. At the coastguard station on the Island, overlooking the bay, Norman Laity had little to do but observe the weather and wait for the end of his watch.

It was one and a half hours after low water and in the harbour four young men, aged between 14 to 21 years, were busy moving around a 17 foot kestrel sailing dinghy high and dry at its moorings. I could see that they were attempting to raise the sails and this made me wonder what their intentions were. So I decided to stay and watch their efforts and the progress of the advancing tide towards their position. I was not worried because inside the harbour the waters were sheltered from the wind and conditions were quite pleasant.

By three o'clock the dinghy was afloat, and through my binoculars I could see that only one teenage boy out of the four had a life jacket on. The sails of the boat were not properly raised and bellied out in the wind. I still was not alarmed, thinking that the craft was going to sail inside the harbour. Surely they were not going to sail out into the bay in the prevailing weather? Therefore imagine my surprise when just ten minutes later the dinghy slipped its mooring and headed straight out of the harbour.

At the coastguard station Norman was flabbergasted as I told him that the dinghy was now leaving the harbour and he would shortly be seeing it heading towards the Hayle river estuary. We immediately mustered the very best inshore lifeboat team available at that time. A fifteen foot swell was running at the river mouth and conditions were extreme for the launching of the inshore lifeboat. So together with Eric Ward, the senior and most experienced inshore lifeboatman, Philip Allen and William Thomas (both coxswains in their own right) were tasked to proceed as crew as soon as needed.

Just after half past three, and in consultation with Norman Laity, we decided that it would not be possible for the dinghy to return to the harbour in the prevailing weather conditions. Already being badly handled, the kestrel dinghy was swerving across the waves in an alarming manner and could have filled with water at any time. Therefore two minutes later the inshore lifeboat was launched from the lifeboat house in the harbour car park.

Norman was well aware that he had to keep the dinghy in sight with the large set of fine binoculars at the coastguard lookout. Already the craft was disappearing from view behind the waves at times. Eric and his crew, close to sea level, could not see the boat at all as they raced towards Hayle. This caused Norman at the coastguard lookout quite a problem, as he concentrated on watching the erratic movement of the sailing dinghy and passing its position to the inshore lifeboat. Added to which, his phone was ringing with demands from the newly opened coastguard station at Falmouth for information. His answers were brief and to the point as he had a more important duty at that time; watching the unfolding drama in front of him. Coolly, he directed the lifeboat straight to the dingy. As he watched, the 17 foot boat disappeared behind a large wave and capsized. In fact, it had turned out of control through a right angle across the breaking sea and then turned over onto a sandbank which formed the river bar at that time. Due to Norman's excellent work, only seconds later the inshore lifeboat broke through the waves and could see the very dangerous situation rapidly developing in front of them. As the dinghy overturned, the mast had driven into the sand and then snapped off at its base. The boat rolled over the protruding mast and dumped three of the young men into the water. The fourth was trapped inside the hull semi-conscious and rapidly drowning. The rigging now acted as a connection to the mast which was well buried in the sand so preventing the boat drifting away. However, the boat was being lifted some 15 feet by the waves and then crashing down onto the sand again.

At the lifeboat house I had been joined by the senior watch-keeping auxiliary coastguard at St. Ives, Laurie Milton. As we listened on the radio we heard Eric Ward call for radio silence and express the opinion – and I quote: "This is serious!"

Eric was not one to exaggerate and I asked Laurie to get a helicopter at once in case of trouble with the lifeboat as well. He asked Norman to radio the coastguard liaison officer Robbie Robbins, on duty at Culdrose that day; and the helicopter was soon on its way.

Meanwhile, in a very skilful and brave action, Eric had driven the lifeboat alongside the stricken dinghy. However, as they pulled the four boys aboard, the propeller of the lifeboat fouled the rigging of the wreck. Philip Allen jumped over the side to assist Eric in freeing the propeller, and William was pulling survivors aboard and giving them medical assistance. While helping Eric, Philip, sometimes swimming and sometimes wading, was violently thrown against the engine and damaged his ribs. After getting him back aboard, Eric realised they had another problem. Two of the seven airtight sections, including the keel, had been punctured, and with the weight of seven now on board, the lifeboat was only capable of half speed.

None-the-less, and not without a little luck, the lifeboat came safely through the breaking surf and, with the helicopter keeping an anxious watch from above, made its way slowly to St. Ives harbour in the very poor conditions. There we had organised a police car with blankets and the heaters going flat out to revive the casualties, while we waited for an ambulance to take two of them and Philip to West Cornwall Hospital. They were then released later in the day none the worse for their ordeal.

Later, at the lifeboat station, we were busy with the two launchers, Tommy Cocking Jr and John Stevens, organising a relief inshore lifeboat to be delivered to St. Ives as soon as possible. I then congratulated Eric Ward and the crew, as well as William, Norman and Laurie, on a really wonderful service. We made it known to the press, including Radio Cornwall, just how much we appreciated the coastguards' work and then went off to our homes well pleased with our efforts.

Imagine our distress then, when we learned that Norman was facing a disciplinary enquiry at St. Ives that night. It seemed that proper procedures had not been followed in summoning the helicopter. As it happened, the auxiliaries had not been told of new guidelines issued following the recent opening of Falmouth Coastguard Station. Soon many of his fellow watchkeepers were taking his side and the row escalated; until a few days later when a coastguard officer from Falmouth, at the dead of night, changed the locks on the St. Ives lookout, and the Regional Commander of Coastguards announced that the auxiliaries concerned were locked out and dismissed.

I must say that I still feel sad at this outcome. Gerry Steed, one of those affected, was convinced it was a ploy to close the station, and in due course that was the outcome. You can contrast the treatment of volunteers by the Royal National Lifeboat Institution, who honoured Eric Ward with a silver medal and his crew with Velum awards. Norman and his fellow coastguards were treated with contempt by a service which should have known better. I believe Norman should have been honoured, at least with a commendation.

Today Coastwatch has the awesome responsibility of keeping a visual watch from the Island. It is to be hoped that now the procedures and communication between lookout, coastguard and lifeboat have been worked out and will stand the test of time.

21

Heroic Bravery in a Sad Story

July 15th 1982 was one of those overcast summer days with a light north-west wind at St. Ives. To the casual observer the sea looked relatively smooth and it was only when people went down to the beach that they discovered a really strong swell breaking very close to the shore. Out in the Atlantic Ocean, far away, a storm was leaving its mark in a heavy ground sea which was producing the breaking swell. In the deep water offshore the action was slow and it only moved the ships and boats at sea fairly gently. However, to the seasoned observer, along the coast to the west of St. Ives swells of ten feet and more in height could be seen crashing onto the rocks and sending up clouds of spray at sea level.

At the lifeboat house, shortly after 9am, the coxswain Tommy Cocking Sr was polishing the gleaming brass-work on the lifeboat whilst listening to the various local fishing boats exchanging information on fish prices and other local topics of interest on the lifeboat radio.

Some three and a half miles west of St. Ives the fishing vessel *Josephine* was on its way home, having hauled its fishing gear and gathered the catch of crabs and lobsters. On board were Jack Ransome and his son Tom, and true to their nick name 'Radio Ransome', they were discussing the latest warship arrivals home from the Falklands War.

In the meantime I was on the phone to a senior coastguard in Falmouth, complaining of poor reception that seemed to prevent them hearing those on the inshore lifeboat when it was at sea west of St. Ives.

Just after 9.15am Tommy noticed that Tom Ransome was now silent and the other fishing boat was calling him to see if he was all right. As the coxswain listened, Tom Ransome came on the air with the news that they had sighted a yacht on the rocks just east of Navax Point (some three miles west of St. Ives) and close by was a life raft and it looked like someone might be in it. "It's impossible to get anywhere near it in this swell," he remarked.

Tommy Cocking at once phoned me but my phone was engaged, of course, because I was still talking to the Falmouth coastguard; while in the meantime Tom Ransome was contacting Falmouth coastguard himself.

At this time we had our own new communication system, with three hand radio sets working on a private VHF channel as well as several receivers. It was always switched on and the mechanic, head launcher and tractor driver, along with the duty inshore lifeboatmen, could all hear me talking when Tommy finally made contact using this method. So at 9.25am they all heard the coxswain report the yacht aground in the area close to the Western Carracks or Seal Island. Of course, his message interrupted my conversation with the officer at Falmouth coastguard and I could hear him demanding to know what in heaven's name was going on. I ordered the immediate launch of the inshore lifeboat and placed the main lifeboat crew of *Frank Penfold Marshall* on standby, to follow as soon as the facts were fully clear. My coastguard contact was clearly astounded as he had heard no such reports of a wreck in the area. Following the end of our conversation he immediately ordered the launch of a helicopter from the Royal Naval Air Station at Culdrose.

Meanwhile helmsman Eric Ward and crew men Tommy Cocking Jr and John Stevens, together with T. Carter and N. Perkin as launchers, had got the inshore lifeboat *Lion Cub 1* underway in three minutes, and by 9.27am they were on their way around the Island and heading westwards at full speed.

116

In order to make the best progress Eric kept the lifeboat well inshore and out of the strong flood tide now in full spate. He was already aware of the dangerous conditions and requested back up from the larger lifeboat.

So by 9.51am Tommy Cocking Sr, together with his crew of William Cocking, Ian Tanner, Ian Kemp and Stephen Trevorrow, were also on their way westwards in the *Frank Penfold Marshall* from St. Ives. By this time Eric had been in communication with the fishing boat *Josephine* and was aware that inside the wreck its inflatable life raft was floating with its canopy up. Tom Ransome was of the opinion that either the wreck or the life raft could contain a survivor.

Lion Cub 1 arrived at the scene at 9.52am, and it was all too clear to the lifeboat crew that the situation was very dangerous indeed. Eric cautiously approached the yacht as close as possible, but soon became convinced that he could not get his craft directly up to the wreck due to the rocks all around. Ten foot high waves were breaking around it and any direct approach would smash the lifeboat, leaving it to the same fate as the unfortunate yacht. So with outstanding skill and with true regard for the safety of his crew he turned the lifeboat until it headed into the swell just outside the breaking surf, then on his order Tommy, with John's help, dropped the lifeboat's anchor. After making very sure it was holding the boat against the surf, Eric began to back his command into the breakers' surf towards the wreck.

On either side of his course to the yacht black weed covered rocks would appear as the swell rushed past. Three times the frail rubber craft landed on top of these rocks as the conditions knocked it sideways. Each time Eric lifted the outboard engine just in time to avoid damage to the propeller. On the third occasion, as the anchor now holding firmly plucked the boat back off the rock, Eric fell over and nearly lost control. However, with considerable courage he held on to the engine tiller and was able to regain control of the lifeboat almost immediately. Each time the boat grounded it filled with water, then as the boat came afloat once more the water cleared, allowing the attempted rescue to proceed.

By 10am the lifeboat had got alongside the yacht *Lady Bird*. The crew could see that the cockpit and cabin were empty.

The *Lady Bird* was now breaking up with the battering it was getting so, certain that no one was aboard, they attempted to get out to safety once more. As Eric and the crew came clear, the biggest wave of the whole rescue swept the lifeboat once more onto the rocks. This time they were not as lucky as on the previous occasions because the lifeboat did not come clear on the backwash and as it dropped the engine jammed in a large crevice of the rock. For two long minutes the boat remained marooned before another large wave pounded in. Waiting for this chance and unable to clear the engine, Eric ordered the two crew members to hold the anchor and use the force of the wave to dislodge the boat and engine. Then, as the huge weight of water washed around the boat, the force of water working against the well grounded anchor jerked the boat clear of the rock, along with its engine. Now with the duel force of the receding water and the feeble power of a bent propeller, the inshore lifeboat was able to clear the surf line and back out to deeper water. A little time later a helicopter from Culdrose air station (still camouflaged from the Falklands war) had arrived on the scene. The crew checked out the life raft and found it to be empty. Then they hovered over the rapidly disintegrating yacht for a final check to see if anything appeared in the surf.

Meanwhile the lifeboat *Frank Penfold Marshall* had arrived and later, joined by the helicopter, started a sea search to try and find the occupant of the *Lady Bird*. By 10.35am Eric and his crew were able to reach the waiting fishing vessel *Josephine* and accept a tow back to St. Ives.

At the St. Ives Lifeboat Station we had been trying out a new outboard motor, so we were able to pull the boat up, take off the old engine and fit the new experimental one, allowing the same crew to return to the rescue effort. So just seven minutes later they were on their way back at full speed.

By 1.15pm nothing had been found despite the efforts of several fishing boats, the helicopter and two lifeboats, so the search was called off.

On the 28th of July, some thirteen days later, the inshore lifeboat, under Helmsman William Thomas and crewmen S. Trevorrow and A. Woodward, recovered a body in St. Ives Bay. It turned out to be a very well known surgeon from South Wales and the missing yachtsman from the *Lady Bird*.

In the RNLI honours presented in 1983, Eric Ward received a bar to his silver medal gained earlier that year on Hayle bar. The Duke of Kent commented afterwards when he met Eric: "That was a hairy one, but very courageous just the same." However, it was the comments made by the actor Leslie Crowther that really stuck in mind when we visited him backstage after seeing the show 'Oliver'. Twelve lifeboatmen were all standing around him in a half circle and, after introductions, he said:

"I don't understand. There are twelve lifeboatmen here but the RNLI are presenting thirteen medals tomorrow?"

"Well," I said, "Eric has two medals."

"Which station?" asked Leslie.

"St. Ives," was the answer.

"Ah, that explains it. St. Ives is a very special town; just the place for a real Cornish hero. Well done, sir."

I must say that Eric not only showed the greatest skill and courage in trying to save the yachtsman, but also never lost site of the duty of anyone in charge of a boat or ship to secure the safety of his own crew. Once again, I repeat that I was, and still am, proud of all the men who so faithfully served the Royal National Lifeboat Institution in my time as secretary of the St. Ives station.

22

Busy Times
and a Christmas Bonus

Mike Sutherland was to serve as a Mount's Bay pilot with me from 1979 to 1983. During that time the pilotage area experienced its busiest time for many years.

Of particular note were 30 very large fishing and processing vessels that visited the bay. Although mostly at anchor, some of the smaller ones used the port of Penzance, and in all they helped us pay our way in the pilotage and boat tending business. To us came the work of landing men for doctors and dentists and various other reasons. In return for this work we placed free newspapers on board each vessel when they were in the bay.

At this time these fish factory ships were processing large catches of mackerel. On one occasion in 1980 one of the Directors of the Mars fishing company (who owned the factory vessel *Junella* which was involved in the *Fast Bird 2* incident in St. Ives Bay) visited our lookout on Newlyn south pier. We were to transport him to one of the company's fishing vessels in the anchorage. While waiting for our boat to complete another task he noticed the pile of newspapers ready to go to the vessels in the bay.

"Where are those papers going?" he asked. "Not to our ships, I hope."

I mildly replied that we supplied them to all the vessels in the bay for free.

The tug *Willem Barendsz*.

Light vessels and the coaster *Lady Sylvia* in Penzance
for refit in busier days, 1987.

MV *Roy Clemo* entering Penzance Harbour.

The end of a long day at Newlyn: Eric with Colin Downing, 1986.

CAPTAIN P. F. MASON CBE FNI

TELEPHONE:
01-480 6601

P.C. 4083

TRINITY HOUSE,
LONDON, EC3N 4DH.

24th March, 1986.

Dear Mr. Kemp

m.v. "Roy Clemo"

I refer further to your letter and report of the incident involving "Roy Clemo" whilst in your charge on 14th February, 1986.

This matter has been considered by the Pilotage Executive who have noted the exemplary manner in which you handled the situation. The Executive commends you on the action taken which resulted in the damage being much less than it could have been.

The Sub-Commissioners of Pilotage have been advised that no further action on this incident is contemplated.

Yours sincerely,

E. Kemp, Esq.,
Runnelstone,
Ayr,
ST. IVES,
Conrwall.

c.c.   Sub-Commissioners of Pilotage
       for the PENZANCE Pilotage District.

Letter from Captain Peter Mason of Trinity House regarding events surrounding the MV *Roy Clemo*, 1986.

Eric's son Jeremy helping to refit MCV *Fanafrost*.

The television team preparing for Songs of Praise prior to the
broadcast from St. Ives harbour in which Eric took part.

Eric with the Songs of Praise team at Newlyn quarry workings.

Towing the disabled coaster MV *Rocquaine* into
Penzance Harbour. Eric at the helm of pilot boat *Vestal*.

The tug *Proceed* towing the paddle steamer *Waverley*.

The paddle steamer *Waverley* at St. Ives.

Newlyn Harbour South Pier in 1988 taken from
pilot boat *Medway*.

Medway entering Newlyn Harbour.
Coxswain Steven Madron at the wheel.

TRINITY HOUSE,
LONDON, EC3N 4DH.

P.C. 4196

26th January, 1988

Dear Mr. Kemp,

<u>M.V. "ROBRIX"</u>

    I refer to your report of the incident involving the "Robrix" whilst in your charge on 3rd December 1987, and can inform you that this matter was considered by an Elder Brother, a member of the Pilotage Executive, and the matter marked Read, No Further Action. The Sub-Commissioners have been informed accordingly.

    However, the Pilotage Executive consider that your actions in bringing the "Robrix" safely to berth with minimal damage to property and thankfully with no injury to persons, are worthy of commendation on a job very well done in what were clearly very difficult and hazardous conditions.

        Yours sincerely,

Peter Mason

E. Kemp Esq.,
Runnelstone,
Ayr,
ST. IVES,
Cornwall.

c.c. The Sub-Commissioners of Pilotage
    for the PENZANCE Pilotage District.

Letter from Captain Peter Mason of Trinity House
regarding events surrounding the *Rob Rix*.

"Oh no you don't," replied the now irate man. "Our company will be charged in the end, I am sure."

My protests were to no avail so the papers were left behind. Just the same, next time the vessel arrived in the bay the crew got the newspapers as usual.

On another occasion we were asked to place an Elder Brother of Trinity House, Captain Dickens, aboard one of the Mars ships for three days of fishing experience.

Captain Dickens had a great deal of authority in Trinity House, and could be a very difficult man to satisfy. He was acting for an insurance company at the time, and knew me well from my time in the Trinity House Steam Vessel Service. The day before he was due to board we made three separate trips to the vessel taking out special food, linen and other comforts for their guest.

Next day a strong southerly wind made conditions very difficult for our task. The fishing vessel was anchored and swinging across the waves as we came alongside in the pilot boat *Medway*.

As we approached the boat we all warned Captain Dickens not to jump on the ladder until we were sure it was safe. However, he ignored the advice and as the pilot boat approached the ladder he jumped. Just at that moment a huge wave broke around the bow of the fishing vessel and the Elder Brother fell short of the ladder and into the sea. He was lucky that Lewis our coxswain managed to manoeuvre clear of him and he was able to grab the very bottom rung of the pilot ladder. However, he was then unable to climb up and just hung on grimly to the ladder.

Keeping cool under the pressure, we were able to lift him up the ladder, and it was a very wet and cold Elder Brother of Trinity House that looked on as we picked up his cap from the water and returned it to its owner.

Three days later we landed Captain Dickens at Penzance in a flat calm, and before disembarking he stood on the deck of the ship and asked our permission to climb down the ladder!

j

As Christmas approached in 1980 the prevailing bad weather brought a bonus for the lifeboatmen and pilot alike. To many a mariner and ship's captain, St. Ives Bay has, down the years, seemed like a haven of safety from strong southerly gales. Close to Land's End, it would seem to be a good place to wait until the gale is past and then proceed towards the ship's destination when the storm abated. However, it is for many a trap, and real trouble for those not used to local conditions. One such mariner found out the hard way just before Christmas. The tug *Ardneil* had been a Glasgow based harbour tug but was being replaced by more modern tugs. The vessel had been hired by the owners of the dredger *Pop Eye* to tow it from Cork to Sheerness in Kent.

However, the 300 ton dredger was unstable, unwieldy and difficult to tow. *Ardneil* had set about the task in fine weather on Friday the 5th of December and all went well until the Sunday. On that day the wind had strengthened from the south-west to a force 7 and the dredger was causing great difficulties as it plunged and changed direction astern of the tug. During the afternoon the tow parted and the master and crew of *Ardneil* had the hard and dangerous job of boarding the dredger and reconnecting the tow. While this was happening the two vessels were being carried by the wind and tide north-eastwards towards South Wales. This caused the master of *Ardneil* to adjust his course westwards into the wind to attempt to get into the English Channel.

Throughout Monday the *Ardneil* battled to reach her objective but each time the vessel found itself heading for the cliffs close to Pendeen Lighthouse north of Land's End. On Tuesday morning the tug gave up the struggle and turned south-east to head into the shelter of St. Ives Bay. As the vessel did so, the swell rolling in from the Atlantic Ocean was rapidly increasing, showing that another bad depression was on the way.

In fact, the weather was sealing a trap in which the tug and tow now found themselves. The swell (called by locals, Ground Sea) together with two storms of westerly winds, were to keep the vessels in the bay for a further week of worry and concern. The master, an ex-lifeboatman, came ashore to visit the lifeboat house seeking advice, and also picked up some stores in the town. We could only tell him to keep as close to the harbour as possible and hope to ride out a north-westerly gale should it come. The tug needed a 14ft depth of water to enter harbour and this made it impossible at St. Ives or Hayle. So he had no real alternative but to stay in St. Ives Bay and hope for the best.

Early on Monday the 15th of December I was returning from carrying out some boat duties in Mount's Bay and was listening on my marine mobile VHF to channel 16, the distress frequency. As I approached the town, just after 2am, I heard the coastguard Laurie Milton, on duty at St. Ives, calling the *Ardneil*. He informed the captain of the tug that a local strong wind warning had been issued. North-west winds would gust over 70 knots in the following hours. Already the tug was having to use the engines to maintain the position and the crew had had little sleep in the preceding days. Now, with *Pop Eye* on a long tow rope, the unfortunate master took a gamble, heaved up the anchor and proceeded towards Mount's Bay. Already the increasing gale force winds and heavy swell had built up to frightening proportions outside St. Ives Bay.

As the tug cleared St. Ives head it encountered the most dangerous of conditions. The wind, swell and a strong tidal current which was running at more than 4 knots, caused a vicious breaking sea. This then added to the danger of the very heavy swell of more than 20 feet in height. As the tug battled with the sea and swell the tow wire parted and the *Ardneil*, freed of the dredger's load, leapt at the sea like a startled horse. Unable to do anything about the tow (which had no crew on board), the tug proceeded to Newlyn harbour in Mount's Bay and berthed there on the south pier later that morning. Meanwhile, drifting south-eastwards, *Pop Eye* ran aground on the sand dunes close to the village of Gwithian, on the east side of the bay. Luck had been with the dredger and it had missed the rocks and Stones reef on the way. The casualty made a sad sight, with the still considerable seas breaking around the wreck as it lay on the beach like a stranded whale.

After breakfast that day I received a phone call from Del Johnston, still the ship's agent and Lloyds representative in the area.

"Eric, what has been going on at St. Ives?" were his opening words.

I, of course, wanted to know if the *Ardneil* was coming back to refloat the dredger and whether the crew would need any local assistance.

"No way is the vessel coming back, Eric," said Del. "The master of the tug has had enough. I shall be visiting Gwithian this morning with an owner's representative, can you give any advice on the matter?"

"Well," I said, "speed is of the essence. If the dredger stays too long aground, the sand could bury the lower half of the hull, and getting it off in the present spell of weather could be a very long job. My advice is to get the Wijsmuller ocean salvage tug *Willem Barendsz* [6500 BHP and bollard pull of 42 tons] now on station in Mount's Bay, around here as soon as possible."

So later in the day Del requested my help as a St. Ives district pilot, in the salvage operation of *Pop Eye*.

The *Willem Barendsz* arrived in St. Ives Bay later that evening, and salvage equipment began arriving from Holland the next day. Amongst these were special floats to be placed on the tow wire as it was connected to the dredger, and various special connecting wires and bridles to be placed on board the wreck.

During the day we experienced another south-west severe gale with the wind changing into the north-west before clearing the area on the Wednesday evening. This storm left a very heavy swell of 25 feet pounding on the beach at Gwithian. Overnight the dredger had been driven further into the sand dunes and we were all concerned that the sand could hamper the salvage operations. Also on that day the Dutch salvage master arrived to take charge of the situation.

At once we held a meeting to decide how we would attempt to get the dredger off the sand. At this time the waves were breaking up to 1200 yards off the beach and due to the strong tidal current it was not possible to float a line into the wreck. Our rocket lines were not powerful enough to reach the vessel, so we had a problem. I knew that St. Ives Lifeboat Station had the services of some of the best inshore rescue crew in the country, so whilst the salvage master shook his head I was regretting the fact that our inshore lifeboat was not available to do the job.

"Oh, that's no problem," he said, "we will hire such a craft."

So it was that on Thursday morning we hired a number of our lifeboatmen, led by Tommy Cocking Sr, to load gear into a local fishing boat which then transported me and the equipment out to the tug *Willem Barendsz* at 10am. Eric Ward and Tommy Cocking Jr waited with some impatience for the arrival of their private inshore rescue boat.

So far we had been very lucky, and with a big spring tide giving extra depth of water in the bay, all seemed well for an attempt that day. High water was at 2pm that afternoon and we needed to have the tug anchored off the wreck by then to use the hour or so of slack water when the north south tidal flow was not running along the shore towards Hayle. Eric and Tommy arrived at the tug at 11am and expressed some doubt over the state of the so-called rescue boat. I was for calling the attempt off, but they were both very confident that they could succeed. So we raised our anchor and made our way over to the wreck of the *Pop Eye*, accompanied by Eric and Tommy in an outboard rubber boat. Just after noon we anchored slightly north-west of the dredger and some 1500 yards from the shore. We had to be careful as the tug was 53 metres long, drawing 16 feet of water, and the swell was at times breaking around the vessel which could have grounded on the sand. Both anchors were used in order to hold the tug in a fixed position; just clear of the surf at low water which was due at 8pm that evening.

With the wind still in the north-west and the tidal current easing over the high water, the tug's stern then pointed towards the shore. At this point Eric and Tommy Jr, in their flimsy craft, moved to the stern of the tug to receive the end of a connecting line. This was made up of 4 rocket lines joined together and then made fast to a series of heavier lines, ropes and finally the towing wire itself. This was the most dangerous part of the whole job, and together with the 2nd officer of the tug, I had laid out the line on the deck in such a way that it would run free as Eric & Tommy braved the massive surf to get to the beach. In agreement with

125

Eric I had requested that the rubber boat be picked up from Gwithian beach by its owner, as there would be no way the crew could get it out through the surf once they had landed on the beach. The 2nd officer stood on one side of the line on the deck and I stood on the other. No one else was allowed anywhere near us as we made sure that the line did not snag or check as it snaked over the side. If it had been checked I do not think Eric or Tommy would have survived in that tremendous surf.

Tommy pulled about 50 feet or so on board their boat and then they headed for the surf line. For the next couple of minutes as the rubber boat disappeared from sight we were only aware that the boat was well by the line running out from the tug's deck. All that could be heard was the moan of the wind as we waited with baited breath for the outcome. All of a sudden the line stopped running and a cheer reached us from the bridge, Eric and Tommy had reached the wreck, what a relief!

Now began the long task of pulling the line, rope and wire into *Pop Eye* by means of a small winch on its deck. Eric and Tommy stayed on the wreck to help, just as a rather surprised owner of the boat came to claim his property. He left shaking his head with disbelief that the boat was still in one piece as the massive waves pounded the shore!

In order to get the towing wire onto the beach we had used special floats to stop it burying itself in the sand. This worked perfectly, so after a hard working afternoon with the tow fast, we were ready to make the salvage attempt by 5.30pm. All we had to do was to wait for high water just after midnight. Meanwhile, under the direction of the salvage master, a hired JCB was digging the sand away from the sides of *Pop Eye* to help when the attempt was made to refloat the dredger.

Then just after 6pm we received a worrying gale warning: southerly storm force 10 increasing force 11 within 12 hours. This meant we could be facing gusts of 90 knots or more during the night. Almost at once the salvage master was on the radio asking for me.

"Eric, I'm in need of a safety boat tonight. When and if this craft floats, it is unstable and could capsize in the surf. Is there anyone I could hire?"

"You'll be lucky," I said, "in a force 10 storm."

"Well yes, I know, but you are the secretary of the lifeboat. Can you let us have its services?"

"No," was my short answer to that. "While on board as pilot I cannot order a lifeboat launch. However, I'll ask my deputy launching authority Captain Proudfoot if he would authorise a launch to stand by, especially as Eric and Tommy are still on board the *Pop Eye*."

My conversation with Dennis Proudfoot was a classic: "Dennis, I request a launch of the lifeboat tonight at about midnight to stand by the dredger *Pop Eye*. It could capsize in the surf and not even a helicopter would be of use if that happened in the dark."

"Well you're the secretary, Eric, go ahead," said Dennis.

"No Dennis, you must decide. I cannot authorise a launch or I would be accused of self interest."

It took ten minutes to persuade Dennis, and I was grateful to him as the coastguard did report the launch to the RNLI. However, all was well and we sat back for the wait until the bewitching hour of midnight.

At 11.22pm I watched from the bridge of the *Willem Barendsz* as the maroons were fired from the west pier at St. Ives and by 11.40pm the lifeboat, under the command of Coxswain Tommy Cocking Sr, was alongside and standing by. By this time the north-west wind had moderated to a flat calm and at midnight the attempt began.

The windlass began to heave on the two anchor cables and slowly the strain on the towing wire increased. An hour later, with the engine of the tug at full head, we lifted the two anchors clear of the water, but *Pop Eye* had not moved an inch. At 2am the high water was fast approaching and if there remained no movement we would have had to abandon the attempt.

Then suddenly and miraculously the dredger moved a couple of feet towards the north in the direction of the Godrevy Lighthouse along the beach, and immediately after there was a larger move, but still crabwise along the beach, and this continued for nearly 10 minutes until suddenly at 2.30am, right on top of high water, *Pop Eye* surged off the beach like a cork coming out of a bottle! I should think that our cheers and those of the men on the lifeboat and the dredger could be heard all over the bay.

As the tug and tow progressed across the bay we could already feel the returning wind beginning to strengthen from the southerly direction; it had been a close run thing. Together with Eric Ward and Tommy Jr, I disembarked by means of the lifeboat, and we watched as *Willem Barendsz* rounded the headland and made for Falmouth with the prize.

In fact the tug arrived there on the evening of Saturday the 20th of December. It had been a very stormy passage indeed and proved the skill of the tug's crew in arriving safely. On the 22nd the deep sea tug returned to Mount's Bay before berthing in Newlyn on the 24th. There the vessel took on water and stores and returned to the bay, ready to help any other vessel in trouble.

Following all this the pilotage staff joined their families to celebrate the Christmas festivities. Luckily no other vessel was caught in St. Ives Bay during that holiday period.

It was in 1981 that the Penlee Lifeboat was lost; I have no intention of recording my part in the saga. The subject has been argued over many times. It was a miserable time for all of us in the pilotage service and our Coxswain Steven Madron died in the disaster.

Mike was to leave me at a time of diminishing work in early 1983 to become a very successful harbour master at Fowey. With his help we had enjoyed a very successful period from 1979. By this time I therefore now owned two pilot boats and covered Mount's Bay pilotage for all the days and nights of the year.

The period after Mike left in early 1983 was a very quiet one, and at the beginning of the week of Easter I was really concerned as to what the future of the pilotage might be. Fortunately my luck was about to change. At this time I was using Selwyn Jolly as my main coxswain as well as Leo Downing.

On the 2nd of April, shortly after 7am, I received a message from the Falmouth coastguard station officer, that the French

Ferry *Armorique* was on fire north-west of Land's End. "We are launching Sennen Cove and the Isles of Scilly lifeboats and although your lifeboat is not needed you should be on alert at St. Ives."

I must admit there was a certain cynical pleasure within the man's voice regarding the lack of need for my own input into events, probably due to my having too many differences of opinion with these officers in the past. So I asked in a quiet way for details of the rescue. It seemed one passenger was dead and over a hundred passengers and crew were suffering from smoke effects. To my questions the officer made it known that the vessel was still underway and heading for Mount's Bay. I thanked him profusely and dropped the phone. What I did not tell him was the fact that the vessel had to employ a pilot to enter my district of operation.

As it was one hour before high water I was just able to muster my two coxswains, plus my son Ian Kemp, and get the two boats ready at Penzance before the ship's arrival.

Later at 10.30am I set out on the *Medway* with Selwyn Jolly at the helm and a passenger, Tamsin Thomas (née Mitchell), a Radio Cornwall reporter, on board. I made contact with the *Armorique* as it approached a position near Lamorna Cove, west of Penzance. By this time Tamsin was broadcasting over the air as I boarded the ferry. Alongside us all the while was the Isles of Scilly lifeboat with its coxswain Matt Lethbridge keeping a close watch on my safety during the operation. Once on board I was able to tell Captain Schawlb that there were many officials waiting and I could take over the control of the vessel while he got his paperwork ready, and this was agreed.

As luck would have it the same coastguard with whom I had spoken earlier answered my radio call to Falmouth coastguard station. I was to tell him that I was now directing the ship to an anchorage off Penzance. His surprise at hearing my voice reflected in his now subdued tone, and he now informed me that they had advised the ship to anchor south of St. Michael's Mount. At that position the pilot boats and the lifeboats would have had to travel a mile more than necessary to connect with the ports of Penzance or Newlyn. Needless to say, I did not accept his advice.

Then began a gigantic task to land all the affected passengers and crew and get them to hospital. Both the Penlee and the Sennen lifeboats helped while the two pilot boats carried officials representing fire, police, health and safety, ambulance, the ship's agent, port and council officials.

The two pilot boats now had to operate with only three crew, as I was busy on the bridge of the *Armorique* with radio duties and the anchor watch. This meant that my son Ian had to switch boats halfway to ensure they could safely transfer people on and off the *Armorique*. So once he left the shore in *Vestal* he did not get back to the port for four long hours.

At the Penzance pier the dock head staff helped the passengers and also the loading of ship stores needed for an extended voyage to Ireland. Also on the pier the Salvation Army was handing out hot drinks and sandwiches with the very best of British goodwill.

It was quite an event and we were to earn a month's money in a day, to all our satisfaction. It was nearly midnight when, tired and weary, we watched the *Armorique* sail for Cork and we could return home.

The following summer I once again met Captain Schawlb at a meeting with all the services involved at Falmouth coastguard station to see if we could learn from the incident.

Once again the pilotage was busy and it became very obvious to me that I would not be able to spend so much time overseeing the lifeboat operations at St. Ives. So following the presentation to Eric Ward of his two bronze medals in London, and the end of the disappointing Penlee disaster enquiry, I resigned as St. Ives Lifeboat Secretary to concentrate on my pilotage duties.

23

A Pilot's Grey Hairs

On Wednesday the 12th of February 1986, Captain Brian Jeffery, serving on the MV *Roy Clemo,* a 646 tons deadweight dry cargo coaster, faced a serious problem while on passage from Larne in Northern Ireland to Penzance in Cornwall for dry docking at Holman's shipyard. Owned by Cornish Shipping, a Plymouth company, the ship had just passed the Smalls Lighthouse near Milford Haven and was now setting out to cross the entrance to the Bristol Channel towards Land's End. A freshening easterly gale was causing the vessel to pitch and roll, and the spray was breaking across the deck. Brian knew that, combined with the spring tides, these conditions could set his ship well to the westward and make the landfall hazardous. Carrying no cargo and on its way for repair, the vessel was short of fuel and it was doubtful whether it could make a great deal of headway if it got too far westward. With such a small reserve of fuel on board, his ship could then be in serious difficulty.

With the ship shuddering under him and the propeller racing as it came clear of the water, Brian decided to steer for St. Ives Bay, just short of Land's End. Allowing for set and drift as much as he could, he would seek shelter there as the weather was continuing to deteriorate. Even if he made it to St. Ives his problems were not over. A month earlier the ship had lost the starboard anchor and this was to be replaced at Penzance. The worry that the port

131

anchor chain was also suspect, left Brian concerned as the ship battled southwards through the night. Even so he was tired, and leaving the mate on watch, he retired to his cabin for a fitful sleep.

On the bridge the mate peered into the darkness as the hours of his watch slipped by. The swell began to break over the bulwarks and wash around the hatchway. With lowering clouds and breaking sea running over a southerly swell, he could only hope to obtain a radar picture of the land ahead or perhaps a glimpse of a lighthouse if he was lucky. However, he was in for a shock when the radar eventually showed an echo of land away to the east of the ship. As he could not identify exactly where he was he altered the ship's course in an easterly direction.

Eventually he sighted the Longships Lighthouse on the port bow, which meant the vessel had suffered from the effect of a big spring tide ebbing past the north Cornwall coast towards the Scillies. Now, with the wind blowing at a steady 50 knots from the east south-east, *Roy Clemo* was some 13 miles to the west of St. Ives.

The mate at once called the captain to the bridge and Brian now faced a further dilemma of what action to take. It was obvious that they could not get back to St. Ives, as the shortage of fuel was critical and the tide was sweeping the little ship rapidly southwards. So as she reached the limited shelter approaching Land's End, and before he attempted to turn into Mount's Bay, he made a radio link call through Land's End Radio to me at my office in Penzance.

At that time I had just had an early morning meeting with the Holman's manager and Captain Dave Frampton of the Ministry of Defence, responsible for the Insect Class Fleet Tender *Scarab*. We had cancelled the movement of that vessel from the dry dock at Penzance to the nearby wet dock due to the weather conditions. Across the bay I could see from the office window the waves crashing over the pier at Penzance harbour. Outside it was dangerous to try and drive across the seafront road to Newlyn as the sea was flooding the road and the gardens of the houses facing the bay.

Brian wanted to know if his ship could get into Penzance in

light of the sea conditions. He explained his fuel shortage and the fact that he had only one useable anchor. My advice was not to try, because the southerly swell and easterly wind were making conditions impossible. My pilot boat would not be able to put to sea and trying to direct the vessel in by radio was far too risky. I advised the skipper to proceed to an anchorage off Mullion, near the Lizard Point, where the high cliffs would give some shelter, and where he would be only 11 miles from Penzance when the weather improved.

As the *Roy Clemo* passed clear of the Longships Lighthouse the extreme force of the wind, now blowing at a steady 50 knots with gusts of over 70 knots, was creating a breaking easterly sea while the swell was running across the sea coming from a southerly direction. Indeed *Roy Clemo* had a real battle to round the Runnel Stone Buoy and enter Mount's Bay. At first its speed dropped to just a little over 2 knots as the effect of the ebb tide lessened.

With the extreme movement of the ship, food or sleep was impossible and all the crew spent the late morning on the bridge; while the captain was becoming more and more worried about the fuel situation. Eventually that afternoon the sea began to ease as the shelter from the cliffs at the Lizard took effect. Helped on by a now flooding tide, the ship managed to reach the Mullion anchorage. Even then, although in sheltered water, a large southerly swell was sweeping into Mount's Bay and the little ship was rolling heavily as it waited at the anchorage for better weather.

Brian anxiously stayed on the bridge throughout the evening but the weather did not abate. The wind howled above the ship, and as darkness fell over the scene both master and crew spent most of their time staring into the darkness and hoping for some improvement.

Just after midnight a real crisis arose when the port anchor chain parted and the ship then started to drift out of the anchorage. Brian, already on the bridge, started the engine and organised the crew to see if they could stay in the anchorage with a small grapnel anchor shackled to a ship's wire rope. During this time he had to keep out of the way of three other vessels which had anchored to avoid the storm. Over the next three hours the ship constantly dragged down on the others. Eventually at 3.30am in the morning of the 14th Brian again phoned me at my home in St. Ives.

I had been having a fitful sleep anyway. I could hear the wind howling in the guttering of the house and my thoughts and concerns had me thinking of Brian and his crew. I must admit that the phone ringing at the side of my bed was hardly a surprise. As I picked up the receiver I could hear the concern in Brian's voice.

"We've got a problem, Eric. The anchor has parted and I only have 137 gallons of fuel left. I cannot get around the Lizard to Falmouth and I am at my wits end to know what to do."

"Well, Captain," I said, "the weather has not improved and shipping movements are suspended at Penzance. However, I will come in to see the local conditions and talk to you on the radio from there. Give me about an hour and I'll call you from my office in the Trinity House depot."

In those days I travelled to and fro from St. Ives in a three wheeled Reliant van, and at times on the way to Penzance that night it almost took flight. On arrival, soon after 04.30am, it was all too easy to see the predicament the *Roy Clemo* was in. Mount's Bay faces south and being in the bay the vessel had no chance of escaping from the weather to less troubled waters. The fuel problem made it impossible to ride out the storm or let the ship drift westwards. As I watched the sea breaking over the lighthouse at the end of Penzance Pier my heart sank.

A few minutes later I met up with my boatman Leo Downing and we discussed what was possible in this desperate situation. Leo was quite adamant he could not possibly take my pilot boat *Vestal* out of the harbour, he could only assist inside the piers.

So I called the *Roy Clemo*, switching to channel 12 VHF, the pilot channel, and requested to speak to Brian. He came on almost at once and asked if I had any solutions to his problem.

"Well, Captain," I said, trying to sound confident and not to let the skipper know my own misgivings, "you have three alternatives as far as I can see. You can put out a mayday and get the rescue services to take you and your crew of three off the ship."

"Not on your life," replied Brian. "What are the other two?"

"Well 1 could try and talk you into Penzance, but with the present swell conditions I would not advise that. Entering the harbour would be a very critical time and instant reactions would be necessary."

"And the other?" he said.

"You could call Falmouth coastguard and request the services of the Penlee Lifeboat to put me aboard. I consider this to be a lifesaving service and your call will be more than justified. Do not be fobbed off and tell the coastguard officer that the Secretary of the Penlee Lifeboat, Dell Johnson, can contact me at this office in Penzance."

Brian agreed that this was the best plan and I left him to call the coastguard.

Del came on the phone just after 05.30am and we arranged to muster the lifeboat crew under their excellent coxswain Ken Thomas one hour later.

I then contacted the *Roy Clemo* once more and advised Brian that I would board his ship off Mullion at approximately 7.30am. Leaving Leo to wait in the office and get my boat ready for the ship's arrival, I got into my three wheeler van and proceeded by an inland route to Newlyn and the lifeboat station at the north end of the harbour.

Inside the harbour at Newlyn, despite the bad weather conditions, all was purposeful and orderly as the crew arrived and prepared to launch on service. We all used the boarding boat to get out to the lifeboat, and having donned my life jacket I sat back strapped in a very comfortable chair, watching as the crew started the engines of their Arran Class lifeboat *Mable Alice*.

We moved through the harbour, and some 5 minutes later the full fury of the storm became apparent as we steered into the narrow harbour entrance. The lifeboat bucked like a runaway horse as it met the huge swell running towards the shore; a bystander watching at the time said the lifeboat disappeared from sight at this point. As we neared Mullion at nearly 18 knots the conditions improved quite a bit under the cover of the cliffs. In actual fact 16 ships sought shelter in the Mullion anchorage on that day.

On arrival we passed the Polish cargo vessel *Koscierzyna,* 4443 deadweight tons, just arriving to shelter, and then edged up to the small coaster with two strained faces of the crew waiting to welcome me on board. As I climbed on deck I shouted my thanks to Ken and his crew on the lifeboat and asked them to stand by us as we attempted to enter Penzance. Without them I could not have helped the *Roy Clemo* and her crew that day. I was welcomed with the usual greeting of "Would you like a cup of tea, pilot?" which I must admit was quite a luxury at that moment.

As I started to discuss with Brian what we were going to do, daylight was now beginning to make working conditions a little easier. Because the wind was from the ESE and the swell was from the south I wanted to attempt the passage of the harbour entrance steering a course with the wind on the starboard quarter and the swell on the port quarter.

"Not possible," said Brian. "If *Roy Clemo* rolls heavily in the swell the engine could stop, Eric."

"Oh dear," I said in a confident voice which I didn't feel, "well we will have to put the swell astern and try and judge the wind then."

"OK, if you say so," said Brian.

So we started our short passage towards Penzance harbour and quietly, on the sheltered wing of the bridge, I recited the Lord's Prayer with real feeling. By the time of our arrival outside the entrance it was daylight, and Television and Newspaper photographers were all in place ready to record any mistake I might make. When we judged the time right, we made a run for the harbour entrance giving as much sea room as possible to the east of the pier head to allow for the sideways movement of the ship in the wind. As luck would have it, just before we got to the pier, a huge swell lifted the stern of the ship and swept it about 60 degrees to starboard. I really thought at that point the *Roy Clemo* was going to dry dock on top of the Lighthouse Pier. We put the engine full ahead and the wheel hard to starboard and as the wave ran along the ship's side it knocked the bow violently to starboard. If anyone had been able to stand on the end on the pier they could have shaken hands with our mate who was on the forecastle at the time. We then swept past the end of the pier and, as a press photograph was to show, the crewman standing by the wheelhouse could have stepped ashore. Yet we never touched a thing!

Inside the harbour we had, by this manoeuvre, missed our proper berth on the north arm, and with the wind blowing furiously we swept towards the Ross Road bridge and the boat slip beside the road. We landed without damage on fenders, but as we organised a bowline to be transferred to our berth by the pilot boat, another great swell rolled into the harbour and lifted the ship and bumped her on to the base of the road bridge. A small wall protecting the bridge fell gently over in one piece. Then we pulled the ship clear with the headline and berthed her on the north arm of the harbour. Much to my relief the ship was undamaged but the TV crew filmed the collapse of the wall and made it look far more dramatic than it really was.

Later, as I sat with Brian drinking a well earned coffee, Douglas Williams, a local reporter for the Cornishman newspaper, arrived on board and interviewed both of us. We explained that the shortage of fuel had caused us to take this drastic action and we both had more grey hairs than at the start of the day. In normal circumstances we would never have tried to enter the harbour in such conditions.

It was a little while later that the captain and myself were summoned to the dry dock manager's office to talk to the owner. He was the chairman of the Plymouth Pilotage Service and should have known better. However, he was furious: "Why did you admit that you were short of fuel?" he demanded and proceeded to berate the captain for his actions. My turn came next and all he wanted to know was how much this little lot was going to cost him. I must admit I was rather short with my reply:

"It is not legal to charge any more or less than the fees laid down in the schedule," I said. "My bill will be about 130 pounds for pilot, boat, waiting time and assistance. However, I would like to remind you that the lifeboat stood by us throughout, and without their help I could not have done anything. I trust that in gratitude you will give the Penlee Lifeboat Station a substantial donation."

That ended the conversation rather promptly and we were then congratulated by the Holman Managers, and that made us feel a good deal better.

Next morning the wind had moderated to 30 knots east south-easterly and we were able to undock the *Scarab* and replace the vessel with the *Roy Clemo* on the very last tide before neap tides would have made it impossible for another week.

The final chapter in this story then began. As the vessel had damaged the small wall by the Ross Bridge, I was required to make a damage report to Trinity House, London. This took the form of a written report with wind speeds, distances, speed at time of collision and so on. On the 24th of March, five weeks later, I received an official letter from Trinity House signed by Captain Peter Mason, Elder Brother and head of the Pilotage Department. After the usual courtesy remarks the letter went on: "This matter has been considered by the Pilotage Executive who have noted the exemplary manner in which you handled the situation. The Executive commends you on the action taken which resulted in damage being less than it could have been. The Sub Commissioners of Pilotage have advised that no further action on this incident is contemplated."

I am very proud of this letter because, as a professional pilot, it is as near as I could get to a compliment from Trinity House. Even if it did cost a lot more grey hairs on my head!

24

Burial at Sea in Mount's Bay

It was in 1984 that I first received a request to scatter ashes in Mount's Bay. I agreed but I refused to charge a fee as we were a pilotage service and not funeral directors. Just the same, I made the offer to those that asked, that although we did not charge we were open to a donation to the RNLI or the Mission to Deep Sea Fishermen based in Newlyn.

However, it was in the autumn of 1985 that I received a request from Penzance undertaker Mr Blewett to carry out a burial in the bay. I stopped him in mid-sentence to ask if he had permission from the Ministry of Agriculture, Fisheries and Food. To my surprise he said yes and produced the document to prove it. I therefore told him about our system and he agreed to a donation to the RNLI. It turned out that the gentleman who had died was Mr Horobin and he was a member of the Royal Navy Auxiliary Service based in Penzance.

The burial was requested to be on the following Tuesday and was timed to start at 2pm, with the coffin being brought to the south pier. There was a snag with this as at that time the tide was extremely low, meaning the boat would be much lower than the quayside. The gentleman to be buried was 6ft 6ins tall and the coffin was heavy and large. It had to be carried by four members of the Auxiliary Service down a steep set of steps cut into the granite pier. I had many anxious moments as it was carried down these steps because the pilot boat *Medway* was berthed directly under the swaying coffin. Nevertheless, the task was carried out successfully and the coffin placed on the stern of the boat. Then the four bearers, a vicar, undertaker and two assistants all boarded and we were ready to proceed.

My instructions on the permission document were to place the coffin overboard exactly one and a half miles south of St. Michael's Mount. As this was my first, and as it happened last, burial at sea, I delayed our departure to explain both to the auxiliaries and the undertaker just how I was going to navigate to the exact position for the burial. The reader can understand my consternation when I realised in the middle of my talk that the undertakers were opening the coffin.

"Oh, it's OK," said the undertaker, when he saw the look of consternation on my face, "we're putting lead weights in to sink the box and we are then drilling holes in the top to finish the job. You see," said Mr Blewett, "these are the instructions given by the ministry."

I held my thoughts to myself as we left the harbour.

In due course, after a short service, the coffin was consigned to the sea. On entering the water it drifted away and slowly tilted until it sank head first. Still keeping my thoughts to myself I accepted a very generous cheque on behalf of the Penlee Lifeboat and safely delivered the party back to Newlyn.

Two weeks later I received a call from a reporter on the *Cornishman* newspaper. The conversation went something like this:

"Captain, did you carry out a burial in Mount's Bay two weeks ago?"

"Yes, I carried out a party to a burial undertaken by Mr Blewett, the undertaker."

"Would you be surprised to know that a body has washed up on the east side of the bay near Praa Sands?"

"No," I answered, "there has been a south-west gale since then."

"Well sir, it seems there has been a funny ending. On checking the man's will he requested to be buried off Falmouth and it is reported that he has come back for a second try."

"Oh well," I replied, "it's all in a day's experience, I suppose!"

25

A Fortunate Rescue for
a Famous Vessel

Another incident of note that happened during my pilotage years occurred on the 28th August 1986. It all began when a small coaster, the MV *EOS*, sailed from Newlyn with a cargo of stone for Littlehampton, leaving the pier at Newlyn clear. Later in the afternoon a tug called the *Proceed*, towing a heavy barge, arrived and came alongside the pier; on board Captain Law had suffered bad weather coming from Liverpool and now took the opportunity to let his crew go home to Plymouth over the Bank Holiday. So next day, with the tug moored inside the barge, he was looking after his tug and tow on his own.

During the morning of Friday the 29th I visited my office in the Trinity House depot, checking to see if any work was coming my way over the weekend. Gazing down over Mount's Bay I could see white waves breaking well offshore caused by a fresh northwest wind. However, with shelter from the land, the sea was fairly calm close to Penzance. At noon I had seen the harbour master Martin Tregoning going into the Dock Inn as his clerk went home for lunch. Just five minutes later my VHF radio receiver crackled with a call from the Paddle Steamer *Waverley* to the Penzance harbour master. Of course, I was very much alert to the chance to earn some money, so I answered the call and then switched the steamer to my pilotage radio working frequency.

Captain Oneal had quite a problem, one of the paddle wheels had broken and the vessel had been forced to anchor 10 miles south of Penzance.

"Do you think, Pilot, you could organise a tug to get us close to Penzance for some repairs."

"Well," I replied (not really believing my luck), "I will see what I can do and will get back to you in the next hour."

Right away I motored to Leo Downing's lodgings and asked if he would help me in getting the tug in Newlyn to take the job.

Leo was not enthusiastic. "I am not crewing no tug," he said.

"No Leo," I replied. "I only want you to help getting the tug out from inside the barge – it will take three of us."

Leo agreed, muttering all the time that he would be missing his lunch.

So it was ten minutes later that Leo and I climbed aboard the *Proceed* and had a cup of coffee with the captain, while discussing how we could help. At first Captain Law was not enthusiastic, his crew were at home and he was on his own. Eventually I was able to convince him that together we could operate the tug, and with the help of Leo, get it outside the barge. At that point Captain Law spoke to the master of the *Waverley* and agreed a fee for the task, then we began the job of heaving the *Proceed* round the barge. The captain started the tug's engine, and in the early afternoon we set off to assist the paddle steamer. Leo in the meantime, waited with the pilot boat for our return.

While we steamed the 10 miles to the Waverley's position Captain Law did the hard job of preparing the towline and having it ready to connect with the anchored vessel. I conned the vessel from the bridge and asked Captain Oneil to have a party on deck to get a light line thrown to the tug as we came close alongside. I explained that his crew would have to haul the towline aboard his vessel as we did not have the crew to manage our own deck operation.

When we arrived nearly an hour later there was quite a lot of movement in the sea created by the strong northwest wind. However, the *Proceed* was a very easy vessel to handle and with one slow run we connected the towing wire and held our position while the crew of the *Waverley* raised the anchor.

Then we were on our way back to Penzance with the *Waverley* coming along safely astern. It was at this point that I called Falmouth coastguard to inform them that we were towing the paddle steamer to Penzance. This message caused some consternation at the coastguard station. With no visual watch in Mount's Bay and no indication on their emergency radio channels they were really surprised at the news. They, of course, wanted to know if we wanted any help and I was quite pleased to inform them that the 'Mount's Pilotage Service' had everything under control.

On arrival off Penzance the *Waverley*'s crew dropped the anchor and cast off our towline. Then Leo, in the pilot boat, brought a gang of Holman shipyard workers out to the paddle steamer and they began a temporary repair on the wheel. Following this, with Leo's help, Captain Law and I returned the tug to Newlyn harbour and the barge.

On the completion of the temporary repair I was able to pilot the *Waverley* into the harbour of Penzance on the evening tide. The shipyard was able to make a permanent repair over the Bank Holiday and in the meantime the enterprising crew opened the ship to visitors. A very large number came aboard over the weekend and the ship actually earned more money than if it had completed the charter to the Isle of Wight.

26

Kiss of Death for
the Pilotage Service

It was in 1986 that the death sentence was passed on the Mount's Bay Pilotage Service. The Conservative government gave control of the Trinity House Pilotage to local ports and harbour authorities. In the case of Penzance this meant the well meaning but totally inexperienced Penwith Council harbour committee.

Problems surrounding the pilotage service were mounting. The Newlyn commissioners were only experienced in the fishing industry and the shipping of stone from the port, and I had long been a thorn in District Council affairs, being the first member of the public to question their planning committee in open session. Added to this, it was to be a quiet year and the number of ships calling at Newlyn was declining dramatically. Finally, the charges allowed for pilotage had been frozen and remained that way until circumstances not under my control were to force me out.

At Newlyn circumstances were even worse for me, after Stevenson's directors were advised by their legal advisors to hire me as an expert witness in two controversial prosecutions of the firm by the Ministry of Agriculture, Fisheries and Food. In that case two of Stevenson's trawlers were faced with heavy fines for illegally fishing inside the 12 mile limit.

This all started in the spring when I was engaged in sailing the *Sea Avon*, having loaded 2150 tons of road stone for Newhaven.

My boatman John Pearce called me to point out the skipper of the Stevenson trawler *William Sampson Stevenson* calling and waving from across the harbour. After sailing the *Sea Avon* we went alongside the trawler to see what they required.

"Surely John," I had said, "they don't want a pilot."

On arrival at the trawler the skipper Roger Nowell (well known for his appearances on television) offered me a full basket of very expensive trawled fish. Looking up to the quayside above I could see the owner of the fishing vessel observing me. I of course refused the fish with the remark that I would be reported to the police if I took up the offer.

It turned out that the warship captain of HMS *Leeds Castle* had made out an evidence statement concerning the trawler fishing a half mile inside the twelve mile fishing limit near the Wolf Rock Lighthouse. The report itself had an obvious error and Roger wanted my opinion on the matter. A quick look at the chart of the area and it was clear that there were errors in the statement. I explained a couple to the skipper and it was then that Roger informed me that Mr Stevenson himself would like me to be available in his office on Tuesday of the following week. I would be required to explain my view to a Queen's Counsel. It now dawned on me that the owner wanted to pay me by way of the offer of fish.

So on the following week I attended the meeting and gave my views on the matter. It became clear that the fishing company directors were appealing above the heads of the Magistrates' Court to the County Court in Bodmin. The Queen's Counsel then told Mr Stevenson to hire me as an expert witness in both the cases of the *William Sampson Stevenson* and the *Philadelphia* skippered by Frank Nowell (a brother to Roger) which had transgressed close to the Bishop Rock Lighthouse. This was agreed and I was given permission to get help from the Plymouth School of Navigation, working over a period of months to break down the prosecution case.

We were successful in putting real doubts forward about the skills of the Royal Navy navigators and inspection officers, but then under fierce interrogation by the prosecuting counsel, both

k

masters owned up and pleaded guilty. Fines of £23,000 plus costs followed and the reader can guess who felt the heat at that time. Meanwhile, I had been advised by the solicitor on the case as to the charges I could make for my work. I duly took his advice and that proved my undoing with the Stevenson Company and its owners.

On the 3rd of December 1987 I was to have another bad experience which in some ways signalled that the end of my time as a Mount's Bay pilot was coming nearer. At 2pm that afternoon I was contacted by Del Johnson, the shipping agent, with the news that the MV *Rob Rix*, 791 gross tons, had been turned away from loading a cargo of stone at Dene Quarry, a jetty near St. Keverne on the Lizard, due to a south-easterly gale blowing at the time. At Newlyn we were able to work in those conditions as we could use the anchor while berthing. In better days I would have advised the captain to shelter on the west side of the Lizard as the gale was increasing. However, after a radio call to the ship's master, I was persuaded under duress and the lack of work to have a go at bringing the ship into port. In part my decision to have a go was also influenced by the boatman on duty at the time. John Pearce was a good handler of the pilot boat and had a strong nerve.

By 4.30pm, in growing darkness, the gale had increased to storm force and the captain was most insistent that I should berth the vessel as he had made his way round the Lizard and his company would not be happy at the extra fuel used. John agreed to put me out to the ship and then return to Newlyn south pier where he would handle the job of making the ship's moorings fast on the quay.

At first all went well, and the captain manoeuvred the ship across the wind in such a way that I was able to jump on the pilot ladder and get aboard. We then waited on the ship until John was ready. All the time the wind was increasing and it was a growing concern to say the least. Once we were under way and approaching the harbour mouth, with just a short time before we were due to drop anchor, unbelievably the ship's engines failed.

Newlyn Harbour entrance is not wide enough for a ship to turn

146

around and it was necessary in such weather to hold the ship in position to enter bow first and slide into the south pier without turning. The ship, now without engines, was drifting towards the rocks and the north pier of the entrance. We at once ordered the chief officer to drop anchor. Shortly afterwards the ship's bow began to swing to the south. However, the stern now collided with the end of the north pier.

The captain then went to the bow to help the chief officer drop a second anchor. Meanwhile I ordered my boatman to get the pilot boat out towards the stern of the *Rob Rix* and take a stern line to the south pier. John then asked a bystander, Derek Harvey (who today sings with me in the Mousehole Male Voice Choir as a top tenor), to haul the rope upon the quayside, saying I would pay him later for his trouble.

By this time the ship had hit the pier end, dislodging a shore navigation light. This cost more to repair than the damage done to the ship, by the way, but halted the turn of the vessel. John managed to pick me up from the pilot ladder still hanging over the side and we then took a ship's line back to the quay from the stern. By hauling on this rope, when it was made fast on shore, the ship was moved ahead, clearing the pier. Then as the stern was blown into the harbour the bow was held steady by the two anchors. So it was that we managed to get the ship's stern onto the berth.

Now with the bow pointing in completely the wrong direction (east instead of west), it then remained to get the bow alongside the pier. To do so we had to run our pilot boat *Medway* out to the bow where the wind and waves were terrible. In getting the line aboard we damaged *Medway* above the waterline.

Finally, with the windlass pulling the bowline and slacking the anchor cables, we completed the job with the ship berthed head to sea. This was the only time I ever saw, in 20 years as pilot, such a position reached. Next day we made some temporary repairs to the pilot boat and started long negotiations with the ship's owners in Hull to get an insurance payment. One thing to note concerning this incident was the lack of interest from the new commissioners.

The Newlyn harbour master's only comment was about the

insurance payment for the navigation light. No interest whatsoever was shown in the pilotage or damage we had suffered.

Some two months later an Irish beam trawler, departing from the Newlyn harbour, collided with the *Medway* which started to sink. On this occasion the harbour staff quickly moved the boat with the harbour launch and ran it aground in the inner harbour basin. There I started repairs, and during that time the *Medway* was not able to earn its keep. These repairs cost over nineteen thousands pounds and took some three months to complete. This proved a blow from which I was not to recover.

At the beginning of October 1989 Del Johnson phoned me to say that the small coaster *Betty C* was coming to Newlyn to load a cargo of stone. He then went on to say that the quarry would be closing down. To say I was shocked would be an understatement and I had to consider my own position for the future.

In the first week or so I struggled to see how my future as a Mount's Bay pilot could be maintained. In the end, to allow for the periods when there would be little work available to me, I asked the pilotage commissioners if they would pay me five hundred pounds per year to continue the contract. If not I would be unable to give the service in the future.

It was no secret that the Penzance harbour master wanted to add the pilotage and boat work to his own salary, so I was therefore not surprised when they described my offer as a breaking of the contract and a few days later, on the 10th of that month, I appeared in front of a meeting of the authority. My union representative hardly spoke during the meeting and admitted he knew little about pilotage. My appeal lasted less than half an hour, and the commissioners informed me that they would let me know their decision in due course. It took them less than 24 hours to cancel my pilotage employment. They allowed me a period of time to keep the boats safely in the Penzance harbour basin, following which, with no money coming in, I was charged one hundred and twenty pounds a month harbour dues.

That ended twenty years experience of pilotage work in Mount's Bay. In their final letter the commissioners complained

148

of the difficulty of running ports like Newlyn and Penzance and thanked me in one sentence. In actual fact I had carried out eight thousand six hundred and fifty-eight acts of pilotage. I never missed a ship and was only late on one move. It was indeed a shabby end to half a lifetime's work.

Very kindly, quite a lot of local people supported me at this time, agreeing that I had been badly treated. I had a sum of money granted to me from the Pilotage Act but that soon dwindled away.

On the 18th of October (after I finished) the Penzance harbour master was engaged in piloting the Irish vessel *Inishowen*, 3000 tons gross, to berth at Newlyn south pier. The weather at the time was a fresh breeze from the south-east with a moderate swell. These were tricky conditions and the harbour master did not have a great deal of experience. The ship hit the stone conveyor on the berth with considerable force, knocking it off its tracks. It was never to be used again and caused a lot of concern amongst the public with much sympathy for my plight. I think this concern had an affect on those who had so quickly caused my problems. I was even to witness one member of the public blaming the managing director of the dry dock during the following month. So it was with some surprise to me that the Isles of Scilly Steamship Company offered me a job as mate and relief captain of the MV *Gry Maritha*. However, there is a saying that one should not return to old pursuits, and so it proved with the Isles of Scilly Shipping Company.

27

Thanks for a Job Well Done and then the Sack

Captain Gooding eyed me with a certain amount of distrust on my going aboard to meet him. His opening remarks were a challenge, to say the least, as I joined him on the ship moored in Penzance harbour.

"You need a week aboard to see if you can survive on this ship before joining it for real."

As it was I was desperate for a job and accepted the offer; without pay, of course.

"We will soon see. There is a north-westerly gale given out for Friday and the *Gry Maritha* is not called the Grim Reaper for nothing," and he smiled with the anticipation. The ship was just 590 gross tons with all the accommodation in its very fore part above the bow. At sea in bad weather and only capable of 8 knots, it was indeed a nightmare. In that week I was severely tested but I lasted the discomfort and so started for real the very next week.

However, I was now on a six week routine: the first two weeks as mate and subject to the very variable moods of the captain. My seamanship was rusty in some aspects of carrying cargo and I was the subject for his withering criticisms if anything was not to his liking. Instant fire drills and abandon ship exercises at all times were common place. On arrival at St. Mary's on the Isles of

Scilly, I would be expected to accompany him and the crew to the pub although he knew I was not a 'drinker'.

So it would be with real relief that I would assume the captain's job for the second two weeks. Then the next fortnight was a blessed relief as I was away from the whole scene.

My time with the MV *Gry Maritha* was under threat in March 1991, with the captain complaining at my driving of a forklift truck in the hatch when loading cargo.

As it happened, at that same point in time I was to have a real success in the week before Mothering Sunday. It was on the Friday morning before the holiday and I was in charge as we loaded our general cargo for the Islands. During the morning the weather deteriorated and the forecast predicted storm force winds for the late afternoon and into the night.

Waiting in St. Mary's were over 2000 boxes of flowers for delivery to the mainland with the Isles of Scilly Steamship company – however, there was a snag. Some time before this incident a shipping company had started a new service running from St. Mary's to Falmouth. Their ship the MV *Northolm* was waiting in the islands confident that my ship would be unable to cross in the bad weather; in which case they would load the cargo of flowers for Mothering Sunday. This increased the pressure on me from our manager considerably, and I was kept busy while loading throughout the day, talking to a weather centre to see what the prospects were.

I was not to know that our esteemed captain was freely predicting that I would not go. On many occasions in the year he would wait outside in the bay and have the crew out to lift the anchor and move to a better position during the night in poor weather, only not to cross to the islands until the weather improved. So you can imagine that the crew did not want me to sail from Penzance inner harbour where it was comfortable and safe.

Just after 6pm, with the ship fully loaded, we were ready to go to sea. Our proposed sailing time was midnight and I made one more call to the weather centre. I was informed that if I could get through the first two hours a moderation of wind was on the way.

So I told the crew we were going, and I must say they did not like the prospect at all. One threatened to walk off but changed his mind, and so in the end we emerged from the harbour into the full fury of the storm with a full crew.

In very bad weather the *Gry Maritha* was a nightmare with the accommodation almost over the bow. In West Cornwall we suffer very heavy swell conditions which come all the way from America and can reach sixty feet in some storms. The sensation when you were in this accommodation was unbelievable. Coming from my cabin at deck level you had to climb up a steep staircase (or companion ladder as sailors call it) spanning two decks in height. Usually I would wait for the ship to steady itself and then start to climb. After a few steps the fore end of the ship would start to climb at a very rapid rate and at that point you would hold on to the handrails as the motion would attempt to throw you backwards. Then as the vessel broke through the top of the wave, it would drop rapidly down the same wave whilst propelling you upwards into the bridge entrance. At night, as you peered ahead through the wheelhouse windows, you would suddenly see a wall of water speeding towards you, then the ship would start rising rapidly once more forcing you to hang on in the open doorway.

So it was in these conditions that I kept the bridge watch all the way to the Islands, and the actual journey took us 7 hours. During the night I kept getting radio calls from flower growers in Scilly asking me if I had turned back to Penzance. But by 3am in the morning the wind began to ease, and by the time we reached St Mary's it was almost calm in the shelter of the Islands themselves.

Charles Cartwright congratulated me on the outcome of this trip and offered to place my name on the company's pension scheme. However, with Captain Gooding finally reporting my poor driving of the fork lift for cargo handling a couple of months later, Charles called me up to the company office in Penzance and explained that due to the master's report I would have to go. But he did give me a decent reference all the same.

I must admit it was a bitter blow at the time. It affected my confidence in myself and I was to struggle over the next year to put my life back together again. In the end it was my Christian faith that enabled me to survive and find a far more satisfactory way to live and work in West Cornwall.

It was to take a month before I could find work. I finally joined Coe Metcalf Shipping Company Ltd of Liverpool. I was to serve as Chief Officer on two ships: the MV *Redthorn*, 1599 gross tonnage and the MV *Hawthorn*, 1023 gross tons.

My service on the *Hawthorn* was a pretty good example of the very long hours the officers and masters worked on these ships. I joined the ship in Shoreham on the 19th of September 1991 as Chief Officer in the late evening. The ship had just arrived from an isolated pier near Llandudno in Wales. I found a bit of a party going on with the crew singing and laughing and in a very good mood. I knew the captain, Ian Ives, a former lifeboat coxswain when he was working for the RNLI. He was to tell me that the celebration concerned the fact that the vessel would be staying for the weekend as there were no cargoes available before the following Monday. "You see," he said, "we've not spent a full day and night in port in the last month."

Following my long train journey from Newcastle after leaving the *Redthorn* I ignored the celebrations. Then after taking over from the former chief officer, I turned in and got a good night's sleep.

Next morning the dockers arrived after we had opened the hatches, and began discharging the cargo of stone. Ian left me in charge of the ship and went ashore to buy food, leaving instructions to see the cargo holds cleaned as the cargo disappeared. All was going well for the first hour, then the ship's agent came on board asking for the captain. I informed him that the captain was ashore and said I could take a message.

"Fine," he said. "Give my apologies. The company has sent orders for you to sail this evening for Calais where you have a cargo of coal for Dundalk in Southern Ireland."

The mood changed as soon as the crew knew about the revised schedule, and the complaints came throughout the day as we prepared the holds for another cargo. We had the ship ready for sea at 4.30pm, and after an evening meal we took our positions to move the ship out of the dock's system and through the locks with a local pilot on board. This move was to take over two hours and it was 9pm before I was able to get a short sleep.

At midnight I was on watch in the busy Channel shipping lanes until 6am next morning. At 6.30am the Calais pilot came aboard and we entered that port and began loading the cargo under my supervision. The captain was busy with port officials and paperwork and we both worked throughout the day until the cargo was loaded at 4pm, then we made the ship ready for sea and awaited the pilot who came at 6pm.

The ship moved out over the next hour and finally I was able to snatch an evening meal and sleep until midnight, at which time I commenced another six hour watch in one of the busiest shipping lanes in the world. I was on watch by myself and I was to find myself in this position many times in the next month.

Three weeks later we had loaded another cargo of stone in North Wales, and after sailing at midnight the weather began to get really bad as we rounded the far north-west part of Wales.

The wind was coming from the north-west and it quickly became a storm of over 50 miles an hour. The captain directed the course of the ship across to the Irish side of the Channel but this was only to give us temporary shelter as we proceeded southwards. All too soon we would be clear of the Irish coast and the full blast of the storm would make our passage towards Land's End almost impossible.

At this time I was very tired and was forced to tell Ian that I was not in any condition to face such an ordeal without sleep. If he insisted on my staying awake, I informed him I would have to write my opinion in the ship's logbook and that I would not be responsible for what happened. Ian was a good seaman and he readily agreed to anchor off the south coast of Ireland close to Rosslare. We then had a glorious thirty-six hour rest before setting of for Newhaven once more.

Following this cargo we loaded grain in Southampton for Dublin and gained a night in port there. Then to our delight we were delayed in Dublin for two days and I even managed to get to a Methodist Church that Sunday – a real luxury. Not long after this, on the 19th of October, I left the ship again in Shoreham and had a month at home.

28

My Last Command

At Christmas there was a demand for ships' masters, and on the 8th of December I left London by air to travel to Trieste. There I was to join the MV *Leslie Jane C*, owned by the Carisbrooke Shipping Company. I admit I wondered what kind of company would ask me to pay my own fare. However, the agent in Italy did pay it back when I arrived.

A short journey to the nearby port gave me my first view of my latest and last command. The vessel was a modern one of 1299 gross tons, it carried 3300 tons weight of cargo fully loaded for summer conditions. The design enabled the vessel to travel along rivers with the masts and ship's bridge dropping down to main deck level. This then enabled the ship to pass under low road and railway bridges. At sea the bridge could only be entered from one ladder on the starboard side. This meant in heavy weather the vessel would often have to change course while the relieving officer or crew man came on duty. The same procedure had to be repeated at the end of a watch to avoid crew members being washed overboard.

All the accommodation was below the main deck level, and in bad weather it was very difficult to get the engine fumes out of the cabins. This was due to having the air vents on deck closed to avoid sea water entering the accommodation. Indeed the crew all had trouble with headaches and breathing. At such times I would find most of the crew up in the wheelhouse which was clear of the problem.

Next day we left for Venice, then took a cargo to Valencia in southern Spain. Then on Christmas Eve we left for Foz, a port near Marseilles, where we were to load a cargo of steel for London. On Christmas Day we picked up an urgent call for help. A large tanker had lost a crewman overboard and we were two hours away. By the time we arrived four other ships were searching, and we joined the search for the remaining hours of daylight. The weather was poor and I felt I was almost back to old times as we were joined by a Spanish lifeboat in the search. However, nothing was found and we had to leave without success, arriving at our destination early on Boxing Day morning.

We had to wait for several days before we came alongside to load our cargo of steel, and it was then that I had a difference of opinion with the ship's agent.

On our arrival he boarded and informed me that I was to load 3300 tons of steel. I at once pointed out the fact that the ship was in a winter zone and could only legally load three thousand and ninety tons. "Don't worry, Captain," the agent said, "the ship will not be checked, so you are quite safe loading the ship with that amount." Of course, I did not agree, as my duty was for the safety of ship and crew. If trouble was to occur I would have been responsible, not the company in the Isle of White. Next day I asked the agent where my cargo was to be discharged on the Thames and he promised to let me know as soon as possible. It was a request I was to make at least four times while we were loading, however no answer was forthcoming.

As a pilot in Newlyn I had handled many ships of a similar size loading stone for the London river. I knew that there was a lack of deep water in the Deptford Creek waterway. I had also calculated that I would be getting there as the height of the tides were reducing (called neaps by mariners). So I gave orders to load the cargo in such a way that we would only need a depth of twelve feet to get alongside. With a cargo of 3090 tons this was possible, with a cargo of 3300 tons it was not.

Less than 12 hours after we had sailed, the company confirmed that we were bound for Deptford. They had also worked out that I might miss the tide and might have to stay outside the Deptford Creek for four days. So they urged me to try and arrive early, but this did not prove possible.

On arrival at Gravesend the river pilot carefully checked the draught of the ship, noting it was exactly 12 feet at both bow and stern. On reaching the bridge he congratulated me and informed me that he would make an attempt at high water to get to the berth. This proved successful. Just the same, after I was relieved by the regular captain, I was never able to get another job with the company.

Many times in the next four months I tried to get further employment, with no dole money coming from the government. However, it was the government in the end who hired me as a lowly civil servant in the Ministry of Agriculture, Fisheries and Food (now defunct). I was, following a six month period of probation, to be a Fisheries Officer, grade two, based at Falmouth but often working at Newlyn.

This job did give me some experience of working as a sort of policeman, keeping my eyes on those who still went to sea in the fishing industry. But in reality I was filling time for my retirement in June 1999. In one way it was rather funny as I was dealing with the fishing vessels owned by the Stevenson family, whom I had previously helped when they were charged by the very people I was now working for. However, as luck would have it, I did not have to deal with any problems regarding the Stevenson fleet.

I retired on the 29th June 1999 and have enjoyed a comparatively quiet time since.

Now I can look back on a career serving many different nationalities, but I can say that I only served as crew on ships which flew the red ensign. For me, at least, the decimation of the British Merchant Navy was a bad mistake and I fear we will never be able to see the like of it again. These days I enjoy a peaceful retirement engaged with a few local charities and, of course, the Methodist Church. I no longer lie in bed listening to the winter storms and wondering what the situation will bring. I just turn over and go back to sleep.